Practical hapi

Build Your Own hapi Apps and Learn from Industry Case Studies

Kanika Sud

Apress®

Practical hapi

Kanika Sud
Kanika, Chandigarh, India

ISBN-13 (pbk): 978-1-4842-5804-0   ISBN-13 (electronic): 978-1-4842-5805-7
https://doi.org/10.1007/978-1-4842-5805-7

Managing Director, Apress Media LLC: Welmoed Spahr
Acquisitions Editor: Louise Corrigan
Development Editor: James Markham
Coordinating Editor: Nancy Chen

Cover designed by eStudioCalamar

Cover image designed by Freepik (www.freepik.com)

Distributed to the book trade worldwide by Springer Science+Business Media New York, 1 New York Plaza, New York, NY 10004. Phone 1-800-SPRINGER, fax (201) 348-4505, e-mail orders-ny@springer-sbm.com, or visit www.springeronline.com. Apress Media, LLC is a California LLC and the sole member (owner) is Springer Science + Business Media Finance Inc (SSBM Finance Inc). SSBM Finance Inc is a **Delaware** corporation.

For information on translations, please e-mail rights@apress.com, or visit http://www.apress.com/rights-permissions.

Apress titles may be purchased in bulk for academic, corporate, or promotional use. eBook versions and licenses are also available for most titles. For more information, reference our Print and eBook Bulk Sales web page at http://www.apress.com/bulk-sales.

Any source code or other supplementary material referenced by the author in this book is available to readers on GitHub via the book's product page, located at www.apress.com/9781484258040. For more detailed information, please visit http://www.apress.com/source-code.

Printed on acid-free paper

Dedicated to the Turbo C editor that introduced me to programming and to my parents, for always watching my back.

Table of Contents

About the Author ix

About the Technical Reviewer xi

Acknowledgments xiii

Introduction xv

Chapter 1: Understanding REST APIs.. 1
  First Steps 1
  API.. 2
  REST API.. 2
  A Brushup on HTTP 3
  HTTP Request Methods 4
  GET Method.. 4
  Addressing Resources 6
    The REST Architecture Approach in Addressing Resources........................... 6
    The Query Parameter Approach in Addressing Resources 6
  POST Method 8
  The Stateless Constraint 10
  Summary... 11
  Further Reading 11

Chapter 2: Beginning Node.JS 13
  Quick Popularity.. 13
    "Write Everything in One Language" Approach.. 13
    "A Server and an App in One" Approach.. 14
    The Titans vs. the Public.. 14

The Big Reason: Asynchronous, Non-blocking Model 15

The V8 JavaScript Engine 16

The Benefit in Microservice Architecture 17

Node.js Frameworks 18

Summary.. 19

Further Reading 19

Chapter 3: Asynchronous JavaScript 21

Understanding Asynchronous Programming in General 21

Understanding Callbacks 22

What's in a Promise? 28

async/await.. 31

Event Loop 32

Tying JavaScript with Node.js 32

Hapi.js 32

Summary.. 33

Further Reading 33

Chapter 4: Your First hapi Application... 35

Installing Node.js.. 35

Components of Your Application 36

Component 1: Server.. 36

Installing hapi 38

The Server Object.. 40

The Init Method.. 42

Adding Routes 43

Component 2: Packages 45

Package-lock.json... 46

Role of the Event Loop in Loading Dependencies 46

Summary... 47

Chapter 5: Building on the Basics: Validation, Authentication, and Plugins...........49

Organizing Routes...49

Validation 51

Authentication...54

    Basic Auth..55

Understanding the Code...57

    hapi-auth-jwt2...58

    Making a Plugin and module.exports 59

Summary..62

Further Reading 62

Chapter 6: Database Connectivity 63

Databases 63

Using Sequelize 64

    Connecting to the Database 65

    Sequelize Configuration...67

Handy Tools, Utilities, and Practices...68

    nodemon..69

Models and App Workflow...71

    Introducing Models into Your App...71

    The Workflow...74

Summary..84

Chapter 7: Capstone Project: REST API for Polling App 85

Product Storyline 85

Designing the Solution 86

    Polls..86

    Modeling the Database..92

    Registering the User 93

Authenticating a User: Statelessness Revisited...105

    The Request Flow 107

Creating a Poll Association 108

Delete Poll Associations 110

    Cascade Delete 110

Things to Try Out 112

Built-In Logging for hapi 112

Raw Queries 114

Summary 114

Appendix 117

NPM 117

NPM Install Revisited 117

Checking for Outdated Dependencies 117

JSHint and JSLint for Visual Studio 118

Tracking Patches 119

    An Example for Our Own Code 119

Swagger 120

    The Benefits of API Documentation 120

The Road Ahead 124

Index 125

About the Author

Kanika Sud has been working on the Web for over 10 years now. Her work spans enterprise CMSs in Java and backend technologies in LAMP stack and MEAN stack. She has also worked on open source ecommerce CMSs and UX strategy. Solution design remains her key favorite, while market research on mobile apps and plugins led her to experiment with a bootstrapped startup in technology, called Codnostic Solutions. Find her on LinkedIn: www.linkedin.com/in/kanikasud.

About the Technical Reviewer

Alexander Chinedu Nnakwue has a background in mechanical engineering from the University of Ibadan, Nigeria, and has been a front-end developer for over 3 years working on both web and mobile technologies. He also has experience as a technical author, writer, and reviewer. He enjoys programming for the Web, and occasionally, you can also find him playing soccer. He was born in Benin City and is currently based in Lagos, Nigeria.

Acknowledgments

I am indebted to my parents for the kind of support I've received all my life. It's a privilege to be supported by members of the family when you're busy working on your dreams.

This is in loving memory of my mother, who wanted me to live my dreams, all my life. I've also had the privilege to work with some of the best in the industry, whose collaboration and inspiration laid the road ahead for my learning. This book, and hopefully many more to come, is because of the best in business – Apress, and their wonderful team including, but not limited to, James, Nancy, Louise, and Alexander. Their patience, guidance, and step-by-step feedback for the narrative and technical assessment were invaluable.

Introduction

Research – that's what brought me to hapi. Flexibility, maintainability, and scalability are core areas when choosing a framework. I was new to Node.js, and I thought any framework I chose would be a huge learning curve. hapi was a pleasant surprise, because it gets you up and running in no time. If you're new to JavaScript, worry not – we've covered the ground well. This book is to make sure that you work from the ground up and have a solid foundation in hapi, and if you're familiar with JavaScript, you can always revisit the language and take a walk through advanced concepts like promises and others. We haven't covered any concepts like introducing SSL, node inspector, CORS, and so on. These are independent topics, and various informative articles about these are found on the Internet. What we've focused on is building a story out of a framework, getting all the major corners secured, so that the eager developer is confident enough to explore more and has his fundamentals right.

Before you step into code and make apps, services, and/or your next big project, be sure of "why" you wish to learn coding. That might not seem the right fit for an introduction to a technical book, but to all my learners, the joy of coding can really be assessed if you're sure of why you're learning, and before you get caught in an industry where timelines can get the better of you, it's only fair to yourself to keep the spark of research alive.

CHAPTER 1

Understanding REST APIs

This chapter throws light on building representational state transfer (REST)-based services. Since we'll be learning RESTful Web Services through our chosen language, Node.js, and using an awesome framework like hapi, it's first necessary to introduce ourselves to REST APIs and then understand how hapi makes the process easy. Along the ride, we'll learn about HTTP verbs, resource handling, stateless constraints, and tying it all into representational state transfer.

First Steps

If you really need to know why we're all talking about APIs in the early twenty-first century, you need to understand that while developed software is what the end user sees, at the back end, it's really data exchange. And who is exchanging that data? Two or multiple entities and layers of software. What is the format of such data? XML was a very popular data exchange format in the early stages of data talk – and while we look into the reasons of using JSON as a data exchange format in our capstone project later, we need to understand how typical data exchange looks and how it's different from the presentation layer.

Consider a scenario where we need information about how many students signed in to the chemistry lab on a particular date. Let's assume that the information is in a register with the chemistry lab manager. So what you're doing is asking for a data exchange between that register and yourself, via the lab manager. What does the lab manager do? He serves the information (that's a service) and provides information in the format you want (that's the data set returned) and the medium, in this case would be whatever mechanism he chooses to filter such information from the register. Fortunately for us, the world moved away from paper to digital long ago; and instead of registers and books, we came up with the programmable Web.

© Kanika Sud 2020
K. Sud, *Practical hapi*, https://doi.org/10.1007/978-1-4842-5805-7_1

API

The term API means an application programming interface, where an interface is a medium of communication. When we exchange data, our medium is a service that will use logic to talk to a database or another application layer for fetching data.

If you've spent a fair share of your time in web programming, you already know what the request and response cycle is about. For those who've migrated from other backgrounds, all you're expected to know is that all of the Web is ultimately a request and response cycle from and to a server. So typically, one caller – the "client" – calls out to the "server" and asks for data sets, and the latter serves the request and returns a response in an object over a protocol, a set of predefined rules of communication. After all, all we're doing is talking, aren't we?

REST API

REST APIs and RESTful Web Services made through REST APIs rely on an architectural style called representational state transfer. If you're a beginner, just remember that you are representing the state of an object or a resource and transferring it over the Web. It becomes more of a contract while we are dealing with resource exchange, with a set of rules.

The Web ultimately is a hub of resources. Remember the example of the lab manager? You're asking for resource information when you want data of all students who signed in on a particular date. Such resource information given by services on the Web needs to be scalable, easy to implement, maintainable, and extensible because it's not going to be a one-time request like our real-world example of the lab manager, hence the emphasis on design. A RESTful design performs extremely well where all you need is data to be consumed by a consumer – this consumer can be any client software, for instance, a mobile app. All your handheld apps request some resources, and those resources are served by hitting REST API URLs.

Now there are a few insights, two of which are pretty straightforward:

- The mobile app that is requesting the data should be able to understand the format in which the response is given.

- Breaking the representation tactfully into smaller resources is a good way of creating the response and utilizing it.

In the following URL, you are querying the resource users and filtering them further to a user called Jake Wharton (the field username is a parameter): `https://api.github.com/users/JakeWharton`.

We'll look into approaches of addressing resources and how REST introduces a clean way of doing it. Before that, let's brush up on HTTP request and response objects and methods.

A Brushup on HTTP

Why a brushup on HTTP? Well, it's the most commonly used protocol for implementing REST APIs. The architectural style doesn't know any protocol on its own. It speaks of verbs and activities which are already present in HTTP very explicitly, hence the choice. For greater understanding, it is highly recommended that the reader chooses to browse through the gist of other protocols such as SOAP, SPDY (deprecated), and GOPHER. It serves well to know how these work and why HTTP becomes a more natural choice for implementing RESTful Web Services. A quick sidenote, prior to REST, web services were designed according to another architectural style named RPC. This was complex and not scalable. The SMB market was thus not exposed to the API world. The HTTP reliance has in fact introduced RESTful Web Services to the world of Web and mobile, which is what rules the present.

I always recommend understanding HTTP through OOP (Object-Oriented Programming) – objects and activities. The client and service talk to each other via messages. Your request message is an object, and like OOP, your object has attributes and activities/methods. Coming back to the manager example, you requested the manager for information on students who logged in on, say, January 29, 2018. Your message to the manager is an object in itself. You asked him to GET the information from a register (a URL in case of the WWW) and return a formatted RESPONSE. Along with it, your request is best served when the manager knows that the information is confidential, to be well secured, and so on – which you communicate through request metadata.

It so happens that the HTTP request object (your message) follows the same rules and consists of the following (see Table 1-1):

- An activity – The kind of request you're making, GETting the data from the register.

- A URI – The name of the register or the resource locator.

- Metadata - Settings of the request object, giving more information about the request.

- Request body – In a RESTful service, that's where the representations of resources sit.

- HTTP version – Is the version of HTTP.

Table 1-1. *What a Request Cycle Entails*

Client	Request Object	Response
Mobile or Web	VERB – HTTP methods like GET, PUT, POST, DELETE, OPTIONS	Service layer (REST API)
	URI – Answers the question "Which service layer do I want?"	
	Metadata – Headers like the content length and others	URI ➤ Router ➤ Program method for execution
	Request body – Additional content with the request like files, form data, etc.	
	HTTP version	

HTTP Request Methods

We'll only be touching briefly on the methods here, and more in detail when we use them in our applications. We'll explore two in greater detail, the ones most commonly used: GET and POST.

GET Method

Let's just understand the GET method first, which says that GET me this and that data (represented by parameters) from this URL.

Let's examine the following URL when we hit it in the browser and in a client tool like POSTMAN: `https://api.github.com/`. This is a public API provided by GitHub, and many such API endpoints can be studied on developer GitHub pages.

If you open POSTMAN and create a basic GET request, you receive something like that shown in Figure 1-1.

Figure 1-1. *Request and Response Object in HTTP*

Before we get to the response, notice the tabs ***Authorization, Headers, Pre-Request Scripts, and Tests.*** Click each tab to see what is empty and if any parameters are required. Click Code. Choosing the option HTTP, you get an idea of what the HTTP request object has passed to the service. Keep track of the VERB, VERSION, HEADERS, and URI that we learned about earlier:

```
GET / HTTP/1.1
Host: api.github.com
Cache-Control: no-cache
```

Now, try hitting the same URL in a browser (Listing 1-1). Since this requires no Auth headers and is a simple GET request, you can get a response by directly hitting the URI.

Listing 1-1. A Partial View of the Response from the github api

```
https://api.github.com/
{
  "current_user_url": "https://api.github.com/user",
  "current_user_authorizations_html_url": "https://github.com/settings/
  connections/applications{/client_id}",
```

```
"authorizations_url": "https://api.github.com/authorizations",
"code_search_url": "https://api.github.com/search/code?q={query}
{&page,per_page,sort,order}",
"commit_search_url": "https://api.github.com/search/commits?q={query}
{&page,per_page,sort,order}",
"emails_url": "https://api.github.com/user/emails",
"emojis_url": "https://api.github.com/emojis",
"events_url": "https://api.github.com/events",
"feeds_url": "https://api.github.com/feeds",
"followers_url": "https://api.github.com/user/followers",
"following_url": "https://api.github.com/user/following{/target}",
"gists_url": "https://api.github.com/gists{/gist_id}",
"hub_url": "https://api.github.com/hub"
}
```

Go through the API list on GitHub and see what each API provides. It's a very interesting insight.

Addressing Resources

The REST Architecture Approach in Addressing Resources

REST requires each resource to have at least one URI.

A RESTful service uses a directory hierarchy like human-readable URIs to address its resources, separated by slashes as shown in the preceding text. The format is almost always by convention and good practice:

Protocol://ServiceName/ResourceType/ResourceID

The Query Parameter Approach in Addressing Resources

What we saw earlier was the REST style of addressing resources. For instance, `http://schoolOfDelhi/candidates/1` is a newer way of addressing resources as opposed to the query parameter approach: `http://schoolOfDelhi/candidates?id=1`.

REST is not opposed to using either approach, but I recommend looking into the following scenarios, which are more appropriate:

- Readability – Your URLs are extremely readable in the REST fashion, that is, a directory hierarchy format.

- Coherence – If you need to provide file format information or information which isn't directly related to the resource you are fetching, you could mix and match the two approaches:

  ```
  http://schoolOfDelhi/candidates/1?format=xml&
  encoding=UTF8.
  ```

- Search engine-friendly – Your URL might not remain user-friendly if you make it too complex with query parameters. SEO guides could tell you how to structure your URLs, most often keeping the name of the resource directly after the service name, followed by the unique identifier.

- Initial purpose – Query parameters were initially intended for providing parameter values to a process. For instance, in the preceding URL where we provide the format as xml and encoding as UTF-8, using these as parameters to a service is one thing and specifying the ID as a mandate is another.

Consider this URL:

```
https://api.github.com/search/users?q=repos:>42+followers:>100
```

If you use this URL on a browser directly, you get a list of users where the number of repos is greater than 42 and the number of followers is greater than 100, for each. Notice how the URL is structured; it gives the name of the HOST, the service or the OPERATION, and most importantly the RESOURCE – all this in the REST style of structuring a URL. The parameters that further decide the filters of the resource and are complex to structure in a folder hierarchy manner are presented in a query string format.

POST Method

The POST method helps you to write data to a database using a service over the HTTP protocol.

This is used more often for the CRUD operation of the lifecycle, where you are creating an instance of your resource. Every time you make a POST request, you write a new record to your database, unless you specify an ID that already exists, for instance:

```
POST /orgs/:org/teams
```

This would create a team object every time you hit the URL with the name of the organization. Here's info from the developer docs at Mozilla:

> *The POST method is used to submit an entity to the specified resource, often causing a change in state or side effects on the server.*

The developer docs at Mozilla are again a great place to understand the HTTP object as a whole. We give a whole list of further reading at the end of the chapter. What is important to note is how we make such requests and what the message looks like when requested from the client. With that, we'll just take a sample POST message for now:

```
POST /test HTTP/1.1
Host: foo.example
Content-Type: application/x-www-form-urlencoded
Content-Length: 27

field1=value1&field2=value2
```

HTTP Revisions   In May 2015, HTTP/2 was officially standardized. By July 2016, 8.7% of all websites were already using it, representing more than 68% of all requests then. HTTP 1.1, however, has been the most stable version of the protocol, even though many extensions provide alternate ways of compressing headers and improving performance and others.

Other HTTP Verbs   PUT, PATCH, DELETE, and OPTIONS are not needed at first but are important in the journey of developing a RESTful Web Service. In other words, when you are handling resources, you should know what the HTTP protocol provides, and therefore we will look into all of these along with what are **safe** and

idempotent operations as we go on. We will also notice how RESTful Web Services handle Cross-Origin Headers, cookies, caching, authentication, and much much more. The reason of not going forward with such definitions here is that we'd better understand them in the context of hapi.js and our applications.

Let's take a look at Listing 1-1 again. It's the response body for the URI at `https://api.github.com/`. If you hit it in POSTMAN however, you'd get a chance to observe the Response Headers, Status Line, and so on. A typical response is listed in Table 1-2.

Table 1-2. *Examining the Response Object*

Client	Response Object	Response
A business routine	The version of the HTTP protocol	Mobile or web app
	A status code, indicating if the request was successful, or not, and why, and a status message	
	Metadata – Headers like headers for requests	
	A body containing the fetched resource	

The response in our API object contains 22 headers for the preceding URI (Figure 1-2). All carry various pieces of information, which may be utilized at various levels. Check the **Headers** tab.

access-control-allow-origin →*
access-control-expose-headers →ETag, Link, Location, Retry-After, X-GitHub-OTP, X-RateLimit-Limit, X-RateLimit-Remaining, X-RateLimit-Reset, X-OAuth-Scopes, X-Accepted-OAuth-Scopes, X-Poll-Interval, X-GitHub-Media-Type
cache-control →public, max-age=60, s-maxage=60
content-encoding →gzip
content-security-policy →default-src 'none'
content-type →application/json; charset=utf-8
date →Sun, 15 Dec 2019 16:56:22 GMT
etag →W/"307bf49b7e1b8e6fe4ef622d609665e1"
referrer-policy →origin-when-cross-origin, strict-origin-when-cross-origin
server →GitHub.com
status →200 OK
strict-transport-security →max-age=31536000; includeSubdomains; preload
transfer-encoding →chunked
vary →Accept, Accept-Encoding
x-content-type-options →nosniff
x-frame-options →deny
x-github-media-type →github.v3; format=json
x-github-request-id →CD6F:471C:1AABCF1:22BAEA6:5DF665B5
x-ratelimit-limit →60
x-ratelimit-remaining →59
x-ratelimit-reset →1576432581
x-xss-protection →1; mode=block

Figure 1-2. *Response Headers for a Sample GET Request*

The Stateless Constraint

A very important factor in the REST architecture is statelessness. Each request from client to server must contain all of the information necessary to understand the request and cannot take advantage of any stored context on the server. Session state should be therefore kept entirely on the client. Every HTTP request happens in complete isolation. Previously, there was a way of storing the session on the server, and while that reduced the complexity, storing the application state on the server had various disadvantages including having to monitor the state of the application from the server, which in fact is the client's job. The server is best suited for the resource state, which it returns as a response. In short, your request should not depend on any other request or the session on the server. A web service in REST only needs to care about your application state when you're actually making a request. The rest of the time, it should not even know you exist. This means that whenever a client makes a request, it must include all the application states the server will need to process it.

Summary

The main aim of this chapter was to give you a glimpse of what you're doing when you're coding a RESTful Web Service. You're requesting information, through an API, and you're sending objects and receiving objects to do the same. What is important to remember is that REST is just an architectural style and is independent of any protocol. We discussed HTTP because the protocol provides VERBS that RESTful architecture uses.

Architectures can be based on other application layer protocols if they already provide a rich and uniform vocabulary for applications based on the transfer of meaningful representational state.

When styling in REST, you need to treat every resource on a separate URL. Guidelines for stateless design make the application easily scalable and fast to access. Our recommendations in Further Reading also include a dissertation – should you actually care to read it – which gives an insight into the real need of REST.

Further Reading

Developer docs on Mozilla – `https://developer.mozilla.org/en-US/docs/Web/HTTP`

A comprehensive listing of public APIs – `www.programmableweb.com/api-university`

The REST Wiki – `https://en.wikipedia.org/wiki/Representational_state_transfer`

A paper worth reading regarding the original need of REST – `https://github.com/otaviofff/restful-grounding/blob/master/papers/official-paper-icwi.pdf`

CHAPTER 2

Beginning Node.JS

We now have an understanding of what REST APIs are, and it's time to understand Node.js in a larger context. This chapter covers what Node.js is. We take a brief look at Node.js and differentiate it from Node. The two are often confused or interchangeably used. We start by understanding the popularity of Node.js and how it became the go-to point for REST APIs. If you're a solution architect trying to understand which tech stack to use, this could be the chapter you want to read, considering hot topics like which stack to use for mobile app backend development. We end by looking at the possible downside of using Node.js without a framework and a very brief description of Node.js modules.

Quick Popularity

In a very recent discussion forum on a technically aware community, we discussed why Node.js gained popularity in REST APIs. Before beginning to understand Node.js, we'd like to point out a few trends that modern web apps are following.

"Write Everything in One Language" Approach

Somewhere down the line, the dev community preferred to reduce everything to just one language while making a solution. This is in most of the cases. For instance, JPA for the Java community became very popular for the same reason. Any tech stack, written completely in JavaScript, was bound to be popular and especially attractive for smaller web apps, because you're frequently expecting JavaScript expertise for the client-side logic.

© Kanika Sud 2020

K. Sud, *Practical hapi*, https://doi.org/10.1007/978-1-4842-5805-7_2

"A Server and an App in One" Approach

Q: Now, a server being an application itself...as opposed to one server handling many applications. How do you think that differs or alters performance, and which would you prefer?

A: Historically, it would be one server hosting many apps. But not so anymore. Considering that (i) clustering servers is not the need of the hour, you can slot in more processing powers through more CPUs and (ii) lightweight servers like Tomcat, Jetty, and Node.

Consider Spring Boot. It's like Node.js in that the app and server are one, but at the same time it's different, because what you really have is still a separation between the web app and the web app server. It's just not as visible because Spring Boot wraps both of them together. Node.js doesn't separate the server code from the app code, so there's an even greater potential for sharing resources between the two. Now if you're designing a REST API, Node.js is just the choice.

The Titans vs. the Public

There was a time when technology meant only enterprise-level applications. The world belonged to large consultancies, who served financial institutions, healthcare, and the like, heavy risk, heavy data-driven apps over load balancers to enterprises where technology could make a difference of life and death, not only a million dollars. Welcome, small-scale world for the common public. When technology was introduced for everyday reasons, "lighter" tech was introduced too. When security isn't a huge concern, Node.js easily wins the game because of the sleek way it fits into the MEAN stack. Assembling exactly what you need and plugging it into Read Write Serve is a straightforward task in the NPM ecosystem, thanks to the many packages you have. Borrowing from Object-Oriented Programming, the small-scale tech world carves its own niche, and JavaScript and Node.js lead because their libraries and modules are proven winners for quick solutions when your go-to market plan timelines are tighter. You'd only be glad to use JavaScript for an end-to-end client- and server-side stack in entirety.

The Big Reason: Asynchronous, Non-blocking Model

This is not a book on JavaScript, and hence we cannot dive deep into what JavaScript does and how it works. If you know very little about JavaScript and are still looking to migrate to Node.js and its frameworks from a non-JavaScript background, I'd recommend a basic understanding through reading and videos of

- Call stack

- Asynchronous

- Callbacks

We'll look at all these in Chapter 3 when we walk you through the essentials of JavaScript – just so that you know what's happening when we're working in hapi.js. Please note that nothing in JavaScript is asynchronous in itself. It's to say that JavaScript allows for the asynchronous programming model. And Node.js runtime takes full advantage of it.

Here, we're telling you how traditional models spawn a thread for each request. This system waits for a request to be handled and then processes the next. Even in a multi-threaded environment, handling threads through your application programming is a messy business. How about a nice little world, where the server itself is asynchronous and non-blocking and does not "wait" for a request to complete before the next one? How that happens internally – the event loop – most developers would not need to bother about in everyday REST APIs (don't worry, we'll make sure you know these concepts too). The short story is that asynchronous handling made Node.js very popular.

This chapter is a very short chapter on the popularity of Node.js, but before we end it, we want you to understand the internal working of something called the event loop. In this chapter, we take a sneak peek with a real-world analogy. In the next chapter, when we're dealing with real JavaScript code, we revisit the concept for a better, more thorough understanding.

Imagine a simple scenario when you're cooking at home. Now, when you're on a single stove, you wait for the dish to get cooked. It's awesome that you now have two stoves. But would that, rather, should it limit you to cooking two dishes at a time? And if you were to cook ten dishes for some reason, would you buy more stoves? No. Similarly, in Node.js you don't spawn a new thread for every new request. A process (cooking) requires one thread (one stove). Multiple background processing can happen for I/O, but your app logic does not handle them. So much for the single-threaded environment.

And what if you have someone helping in the kitchen who can check when the dishes are ready while you prepare your batter for a cake and similar stuff? What's that called? Productivity. Remember the help is just checking what dishes are ready and where your attention is required. That's your event loop.

Figure 2-1 provides a visual that could help understanding it.

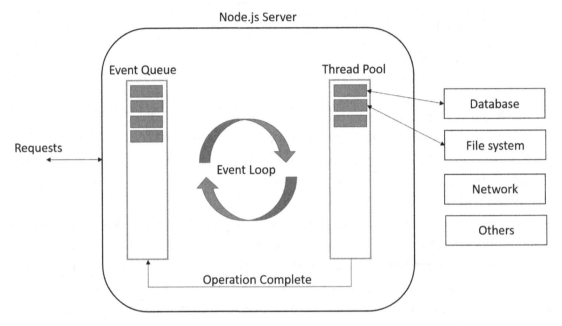

Figure 2-1. *Node.js Event Loop*

The V8 JavaScript Engine

First things first, all browsers have a JavaScript engine which they use to execute JavaScript at runtime. The DOM and the other Web Platform APIs are provided by the browser. V8 happens to be the engine that runs JavaScript in Chrome. However, it is not coupled with Chrome which enabled the rise of Node.js. V8 was chosen to be the engine that powered Node.js back in 2009, and it proved to be just the right choice, as its popularity exploded. JavaScript is internally compiled by V8 with just-in-time (JIT) compilation to speed up the execution. On the Web, there is a race for performance that's been going on for years, and what this means for us is that every engine made for the browser can independently host a JavaScript runtime. It is exactly for these reasons that a V8-powered JavaScript runtime became powerful, while V8 was continuously improved for Chrome.

The Benefit in Microservice Architecture

Prior to the microservice architecture, there was the monolithic architecture, where the UI interacted with one single business logic layer, which interacted with the database layer (Figure 2-2). With a microservice architecture, developers are looking at modular approaches to manage their code across business-oriented modules, for better organization and maintainability. It also has deep effects in deploying and testing applications. The application starts faster, which makes developers more productive and speeds up deployments. I have personally seen this across an application which had to be distributed across seven microservices for it to make sense – and was otherwise a developer's hell when introduced to it. We could isolate bugs better and make a longer commitment toward product maintenance than we would have otherwise.

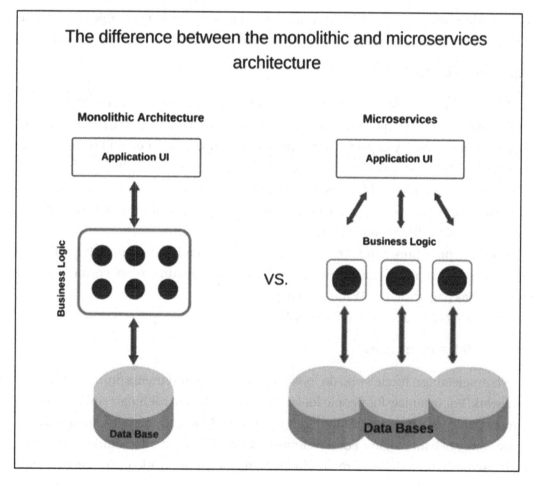

Figure 2-2. *Monolithic vs. Microservice Architecture*

Microservice and Node.js Go Hand in Hand

The three main reasons I'd recommend Node.js for a microservice architecture would be

1. Faster execution

2. Simplified, modular development

3. API support and easily available frameworks

It seems as if the aim behind the use and creation of both the architecture and the runtime is the same – and that is why, when coupled, they do fairly well.

Node.js Frameworks

Before understanding Node.js frameworks, let's make sure we know ample about Node.js itself. Try out a few sample apps and small programs and do visit learning tracks like this:

```
https://nodejs.dev/
```

What we intend to do in this section is to introduce you very briefly to some frameworks of Node.js which are up on the market to catch up with. Why use a Node.js framework at all? Well, you get to work with a set of tools, guidelines, and recommended practices that help you save time. The core modules of Node.js including the file system module and the HTTP module can be used in many ways; and when you need to set standards of a product, you work over and above a set of utilities provided by a framework, not by the language itself.

Among hapi, Express, Meteor, Koa, Next, LoopBack, and many others, hapi does not receive many stars on Github, but it won't fade away anytime soon, considering the backing it has (supported by Walmart Labs).

Here's a list of Node.js frameworks online:

```
http://nodeframework.com/
```

When selecting a framework, do look for your own requirements fitting into the framework. For instance, for people looking for availability of caching, request handling, authentication, and input validation, they can rely on hapi because of its amazingly secure family of hapi plugins. For developers looking for minimalist solutions, Express might also be an option. If you're the kind looking for a framework that enforces a folder structure, try LoopBack.

The reason why we choose to study hapi is because its MVC structure and in-depth control over core modules of Node.js enable the developer to migrate to any other framework easily, once a knack is established with it.

Summary

The main aim of this chapter was to give you a glimpse of why Node.js is very popular. While this covers practical aspects of hapi.js, we'd want you to have a good knowledge of why Node.js is very popular. This chapter was just a gist. We also learned a little about evolving trends in technology – the server and the app in one, one language for the whole solution, and how everyday technology requires quick-to-deploy solutions, rather than enterprise tech with a slower, tougher learning curve. And lastly, our key take-away should be the single-threaded asynchronous model, which doesn't block any resources. I hope the analogy wasn't rough. What matters is what you take from it. We're going to dig deep into asynchronous programming and event loop in the next chapter, practically understanding essentials of JavaScript – and we're excited!

Further Reading

A good summary for solution architects and for developers who get excited by newer technologies, not knowing where to use them! – `www.toptal.com/nodejs/why-the-hell-would-i-use-node-js`

A look into microservice architecture with Node.js – `www.monterail.com/blog/nodejs-development-enterprises`

A good article about microservices and Node.js – `https://nodesource.com/blog/microservices-in-nodejs`

CHAPTER 3

Asynchronous JavaScript

Now that we know the overview of Node.js from the last chapter, it's time to get into some core programming concepts of the language that changed it all – JavaScript. JavaScript is deceptive in that its lightweight structure will make you feel that you're indeed done with the whole language, because you have an app running and returning a response. If you dive in deeper – which is always a good thing in programming – JavaScript can offer a whole new world, where thorough concepts can make or break an app and its scalability. Let's walk you through. We'll just be explaining the most difficult parts of JavaScript pertaining to Node.js – for the most commonly understood sections, we'll leave a trail of further reading and online recommendations.

Understanding Asynchronous Programming in General

Somewhere down the line, in data-intensive apps, you'll realize you want to use resources in the most efficient manner, without blocking a handle to those resources. Now, when do such use cases come along? A massive number of users on the system at one time, intensive I/O operations, and so on. So what do we do? We get the privilege of initiating an operation and it getting handled when the resource is free. Compared to a multi-threaded environment, this brings in a much cleaner, single-threaded, non-blocking way of programming. Again, JavaScript in itself is not asynchronous; it supports asynchronous programming.

For those of us who've been novice developers in client servicing, we have never had the time to delve into the skin of things – it's a little obscure region to talk about what blocking resources means. Well, time for some real-world examples again. Restaurants, anyone?

© Kanika Sud 2020
K. Sud, *Practical hapi*, https://doi.org/10.1007/978-1-4842-5805-7_3

You have one kitchen and one chef. Even then, would you want your customers to wait for the first order to be processed and served before you can even take the second order? Better still, would you prefer a chef who starts preparing the second order once he takes a look at what's in-line (the event loop), midway the first, and serves as and when prepared?

```
//asynchronous call
//whatever code is written here, won't wait for the asynchronous call.
```

Many browser functions are implemented asynchronously. Looking at JavaScript info (`https://javascript.info/callbacks`) would make our point clearer.

Now, JavaScript is a single-threaded language, and to get into blocking calls is very easy if not written properly. For a long time, asynchronous programming was served well by callbacks. The evolution of JavaScript saw promises and generators. We discuss callbacks next. We wish to point out to developers that just like JavaScript, callbacks are not asynchronous themselves. Callbacks can be used asynchronously. Whenever you revisit the topic, look for synchronous callbacks and asynchronous callbacks separately.

Understanding Callbacks

Callbacks are an example of first-class functions in JavaScript, where a function is passed to a function. To understand how they tie up with asynchronous programming, consider the difference between loading a file, reading a file, and some code below it (you don't want that to wait) – what you do here is keep the loading and reading asynchronous, and the rest of the code does not depend on it.

Consider the following examples for loading a file with Ajax and a callback. Note that asynchronous behavior is inherent in Ajax. Callbacks here are demonstrated only for how they are used. The same example can be run without a callback, only that if you couldn't assign callbacks or pass methods as parameters, you'd have to write the contained code over and over again, when instead all you have to do is just assign it as a callback and all your callback-contained code will be sorted in one go – in this case the innerHTML display (Listing 3-1).

Listing 3-1. An Ajax Example with a Callback Function

```html
<!DOCTYPE html>
<html>
<body>

<div id="demo">

<h1>An AJAX example with a callback function</h1>

<button type="button"
onclick="loadDoc('https://api.github.com/users?since=135', cb)">Change
Content
</button>
</div>

<script>
function loadDoc(url, cFunction) {
  var xhttp;
  xhttp=new XMLHttpRequest();
  xhttp.onreadystatechange = function() {
    if (this.readyState == 4 && this.status == 200) {
      cFunction(this);
    }
  };
  xhttp.open("GET", url, true);
  xhttp.send();
  document.getElementById("demo").innerHTML = "<strong>Me First</strong>"
}
```

```
function cb(xhttp) {
  document.getElementById("demo").innerHTML =
  xhttp.responseText;
}
</script>
</body>
</html>
```

Notice the following screens. The first screen (Figure 3-1) shows the program input, a basic button, which executes the script thereafter.

Figure 3-1. *Home Screen Change Content Through Callback*

The program doesn't wait to return the file. It prints **Me First** first, as shown in the following screenshot; and then when the file is loaded, it prints the response. Note that this is nonsequential, according to our code. The third screen shows the actual output that displays after some time.

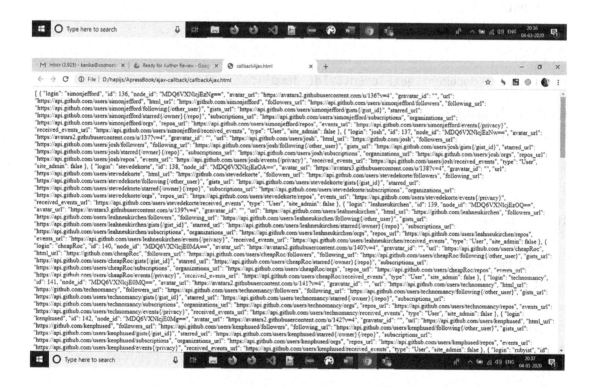

Thus, delaying of execution has happened to when the data was available. Delaying of data can happen after some time has elapsed too. And that's in case of the `setTimeout()` function. For now, just be sure you are clear on how asynchronous programming can alter the flow of a program. Try fiddling with the preceding code.

For instance, we made another code piece without callbacks, strongly giving what asynchronous programming is (Listing 3-2).

Listing 3-2. Code Without Callbacks

```
<!DOCTYPE html>
<html>
<body>

<div id="demo">

    <h1>Check The Console</h1>

    <button type="button" onclick="loading('https://api.github.com/users/
    tom')">Check The Console
    </button>
  </div>

<script>
let script = document.getElementById('demo');

function loading(url) {
  loadDiv(url);
  console.log("Me Second");

}

function loadDiv(url){
  var xhttp;
  xhttp=new XMLHttpRequest();
  xhttp.onreadystatechange = function() {
    if (this.readyState == 4 && this.status == 200) {
     console.log(xhttp.responseText);
    }
  };
  xhttp.open("GET", url, true);
  xhttp.send();
  console.log("Me First");

}
```

```
</script>
</body>
</html>
```

Listing 3-3 shows the output on the console.

Listing 3-3. Output Without Callbacks

```
Me First
Me Second
{
  "login": "tom",
  "id": 748,
  "node_id": "MDQ6VXNlcjcOOA==",
  "avatar_url": "https://avatars1.githubusercontent.com/u/748?v=4",
  "gravatar_id": "",
  "url": "https://api.github.com/users/tom",
  "html_url": "https://github.com/tom",
  "followers_url": "https://api.github.com/users/tom/followers",
  "following_url": "https://api.github.com/users/tom/following{/other_
  user}",
  "gists_url": "https://api.github.com/users/tom/gists{/gist_id}",
  "starred_url": "https://api.github.com/users/tom/starred{/owner}{/repo}",
  "subscriptions_url": "https://api.github.com/users/tom/subscriptions",
  "organizations_url": "https://api.github.com/users/tom/orgs",
  "repos_url": "https://api.github.com/users/tom/repos",
  "events_url": "https://api.github.com/users/tom/events{/privacy}",
  "received_events_url": "https://api.github.com/users/tom/received_
  events",
  "type": "User",
  "site_admin": false,
  "name": "Tom Malone",
  "company": null,
  "blog": "",
  "location": null,
  "email": null,
  "hireable": null,
```

```
  "bio": null,
  "public_repos": 11,
  "public_gists": 2,
  "followers": 23,
  "following": 3,
  "created_at": "2008-02-24T18:44:45Z",
  "updated_at": "2019-12-10T09:21:17Z"
}
```

What happened? The console dumps out the Me First, Me Second quickly, and then when the response is ready and is successful, it's served, still maintaining sequential order. You could also add a timer to the code and see how many seconds elapse for what task – we leave that task to you.

Callback syntax can be confusing for non-JavaScript developers, and the way I keep track of it is to see that the callback receives its arguments – if any. For multiple callbacks, nested versions can become messy. This brings us to the concept of promises.

What's in a Promise?

Coming back to the restaurant analogy, the manager or the cashier hands over an order number – which is a promise to deliver. What does it say? Collect your order when it is ready. Again, execution is not delayed after the first order is complete – we just say we deliver the order when it's ready.

In other words:

```
//Prepare Order and Serve ->
    //Promise 1 - If Order1 is ready, serve order 1
    //Promise 2 - If Order2 is ready, serve order 2(Don't wait for order 1)
```

Again, we are achieving asynchronous results; and yes, the same can be written in callback language as well.

The syntax of a promise is

```
let promise = new Promise(function(resolve, reject) {
  // executor (the order function)
});
```

Its arguments resolve and reject are callbacks:

> resolve (value) – If the job finished successfully, with result value.

> reject (error) – If an error occurred. Error is the error object.

The **state** of the promise can be one of **"pending," "fulfilled,"** or **"rejected."** A promise returns the state and value, though state and value are not directly accessible.

When you use .then(), you're telling your code to proceed if the resolution of the promise is successful. Through a series of .then() functions, called chaining of promises, we use the return value of one into the parameter value of another.

Listing 3-4 provides a new set of code for a simple demonstration of promises.

Listing 3-4. Demonstrating Promises (script.js)

```
function loadDoc() {
  let url = 'https://api.github.com/users/tom';
  let response = fetch(url).then(function(response) {
    // response.json() returns a new promise that resolves with
    //the full response text
    // when it loads
    return response.json();
  })
  .then(function(json) {
    // ...and here's the content of the remote URL
    document.getElementById('demo').innerHTML = (JSON.stringify(json));
  });
}
```

Listing 3-5 shows the index.html.

Listing 3-5. index.html

```
<!DOCTYPE html>
<html>

  <head>
    <link rel="stylesheet" href="style.css">
    <script src="script.js"></script>
  </head>

  <body>
    <button onclick="loadDoc()">Demo</button>
    <div id="demo"></div>
  </body>

</html>
```

The fetch method returns a promise, the value of which is the response object if the promise is resolved.

If the promise is resolved, it returns a JSON representation of the response object. This is passed further down the line, through another successive then() method call. This way, we ensure that the JSON representation is passed only when it is completely resolved. That JSON representation is stringified and dumped into a div of your choice.

The preceding example is a live working example, and you can easily test it in a fiddle. It can be very easily modeled to a restaurant analogy as well. Your loadDoc() function would be a loadOrder() function. You could then serve the response as and when it is prepared (ready – status resolved, marked by your API). The idea is the same here – we make a promise to deliver when ready.

And if one order depends on, say, five dishes and you want to serve the order only when those five dishes are ready, you can even manage it by saying

```
let promise = Promise.all([...promises...]);
Promise.all([
  new Promise(resolve => setTimeout(() => resolve('OrderA'), 3000)), // 1
  new Promise(resolve => setTimeout(() => resolve('OrderB'), 2000)), // 2
  new Promise(resolve => setTimeout(() => resolve('OrderC'), 1000))  // 3
]).then(alert)
```

A detailed study of promises is out of the scope of this book. Refer to our recommendations in the "Further Reading" section at the end of the chapter. Especially focus on promisification if you want to understand how everything you do in callbacks can be converted to promise code. That's for those who want to take their time on JavaScript and then reach Node.js.

async/await

One reason why we're giving you a bite of JavaScript is because these four concepts of asynchronous programming are quite often used in Node.js, especially in hapi.js. You'll see the await keyword in the server.js file, for instance, and to understand what's going on with it, let's understand how async and await help.

First, to the preceding code, add async and await and see how the behavior differs (Listing 3-6).

Listing 3-6. Code for Demonstrating async/await

```
1.   async function loadDoc() {
2.   let url = 'https://api.github.com/users';
3.   try{
4.   const response = await fetch(url);
5.   const json = await response.json();
6.   document.getElementById('demo').innerHTML = (JSON.stringify(json));
7.   }catch(err)
8.   { console.log('fetch failed - async syntax', err);
}}
```

Many users prefer this because it's very similar to how we say things in other languages.

The best way to understand async behavior in the preceding piece of code is to remove **await** from line 5. Try saying const json = response.json();

You'll get an empty brace {} on the screen. This shows us that if the response hasn't loaded and we **do not** use the await keyword, it will not wait for the response to load and the control will move on.

Event Loop

We take up the event loop when we are discussing the entry point of a Node.js application in the chapters to come. Till then, know a very simple definition: here's an endless loop, when JavaScript engine waits for tasks, executes them, and then sleeps waiting for more tasks.

Tying JavaScript with Node.js

In the beginning, before deep-diving into code, you must know that Node uses the Event-Driven Architecture: it has an event loop for orchestration and a Worker Pool for expensive tasks (includes I/O for which an operating system does not provide a non-blocking version, as well as particularly CPU-intensive tasks). The event loop will also fulfill the non-blocking asynchronous requests made by callbacks. While the event loop does not maintain a queue on its own, the Worker Pool does. When Node.js starts, it initializes the event loop, processes the provided input script (making async calls, scheduling timers), and then begins processing the loop. The loop in itself does not maintain a queue, but for a single-threaded language, it helps a lot by checking queues to see if it can take an input from a queue or a phase and process it.

A Worker pops a task from this queue and works on it, and when finished the Worker raises an "At least one task is finished" event for the event loop.

All in all, the modules of Node.js are very well equipped to handle asynchronous programming – which makes it a natural choice for mobile application APIs. You need to serve a lot of data in mobile applications, so quick-to-write and intricate tailoring becomes a good combination when serving data for scalable applications.

Hapi.js

Hapi.js is a lightweight framework which really helped me catch on to Node.js. At an architect level, you tend to see what platforms provide good flow, and hapi.js is one of them. It also keeps messy modules of Node at bay, while you can concentrate on developer-friendly, secure applications:

- hapi offers a rich ecosystem. The plugins available have almost always covered every application design need.

- The guarantee provided by hapi is very strong – for instance, the order in which components are configured is not a problem.

- Plugins can safely rely on other plugins, including the order in which they must be executed.

- Caches, plugins, decorators, and server methods are all protected and cannot be implicitly overridden – so you can say goodbye to the middleware hell. The fact that the framework itself has plugins makes the abstraction layer very flexible.

Summary

This chapter showed you some key concepts of JavaScript that might come in handy when understanding any framework in Node.js, because Node.js itself was adopted for modules of asynchronous programming. As we go forward, becoming clear with concepts and syntax of promises, async/Ajax will help, and remembering the callback pattern as the first approach to solve problems asynchronously will help in understanding why we write the code the way we do. This was more of a JavaScript primer, lest we face confusions in the keywords that might follow.

We also read about the event loop briefly and how it is used in Node.js. The event loop is what allows Node.js to perform non-blocking I/O operations – despite the fact that JavaScript is single-threaded – by offloading operations to the system kernel whenever possible.

We tied JavaScript's asynchronous behavior to Node.js, and we saw how hapi.js is a lightweight framework to use Node.js. All in all, we have the right recipe for a quick RESTful Web Service app. As an exercise, try coding simple applications in callbacks and promises. See you in the next chapter.

Further Reading

https://javascript.info/promise-basics
https://developer.mozilla.org/en-US/docs/Web/JavaScript/Reference/Global_
Objects/Promise

CHAPTER 4

Your First hapi Application

We now go through the essentials of a hapi app, including installing all required dependencies and then setting up the server, specifically the server and its dependencies. For anyone who's looking to start hapi.js and already has their basics clear, this chapter is where the real story starts, because till now we had prepared the environment and background of our hapi journey. Now, you'll get an application with its entry server point, dependency management, and a basic route to start with.

Installing Node.js

If you're like me, you won't stay without visiting the official Node.js docs when working with any of its frameworks. Even though the docs become confusing (and that's why Apress is here!), some things are pretty straightforward. So here you go:

`https://nodejs.org/en/download/package-manager/`

This link gives the most comprehensive set of commands to install Node. The command that I used was

```
yum install nodejs12
```

The number 12 can be nodejs8 and so on. It's for the version. For Win users, download NodeJS from here: `https://nodejs.org/en/`

© Kanika Sud 2020
K. Sud, *Practical hapi*, https://doi.org/10.1007/978-1-4842-5805-7_4

Check your Node installation and off you go! On the command prompt, type node -v. If everything has gone well, it should show the version as follows. Figure 4-1 checks the node installation on the command line.

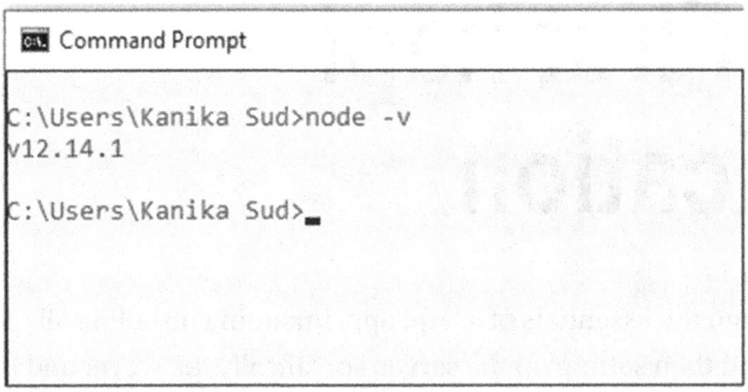

Figure 4-1. *Checking Your Node Installation*

Components of Your Application

In this section, we'll look at the two components that make up our application: the server and the packages. Remember that for any application to run on the Node server, it needs an entry point (containing minimally the start method call to your server object) that the Node server can run on. When running that entry point, it looks for the manifest of the project, a file that contains, among other things, the application/package name, the current version, a brief description of the app/package, and so on.

Let's start by explaining what the server file does in your application.

Component 1: Server

Once you've installed Node, create a directory, say, first-app, and enter it on the command line interface (CLI). Type

```
npm init
```

```
D:\hapijs\ApressBook>cd first-app-demo

D:\hapijs\ApressBook\first-app-demo>npm init
This utility will walk you through creating a package.json file.
It only covers the most common items, and tries to guess sensible defaults.

See `npm help json` for definitive documentation on these fields
and exactly what they do.

Use `npm install <pkg>` afterwards to install a package and
save it as a dependency in the package.json file.

Press ^C at any time to quit.
package name: (first-app-demo)
```

Figure 4-2. npm init Utility on the CLI

```
package name: (first-app-demo)
version: (1.0.0)
description:
entry point: (index.js) server.js
test command:
git repository:
keywords:
author:
license: (ISC)
About to write to D:\hapijs\ApressBook\first-app-demo\package.json:

{
  "name": "first-app-demo",
  "version": "1.0.0",
  "description": "",
  "main": "server.js",
  "scripts": {
    "test": "echo \"Error: no test specified\" && exit 1"
  },
  "author": "",
  "license": "ISC"
}

Is this OK? (yes) y
```

Figure 4-3. Descriptors Asked for Setting Up the package.json File

Just enter all descriptors like name, version, description, and author and confirm when it asks you "Is this ok?" By default, one of those descriptors is index.js – which is the entry point of your app. Change it to a file that suits you. Call it app.js or server.

js or whatever you might wish. We changed it to server.js, as you can see in Figure 4-3. This installs all your Node dependencies. Check your folder again. You should have a package.json and node modules folder installed for you.

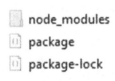

Figure 4-4. *Folder Structure After Running Through the npm init Command*

Installing hapi

The following installs all hapi.js framework dependencies:

```
npm install --save @hapi/hapi
```

The **save** option adds it to the package.json file. Keep noting the changes in the folder structure and the package.json file when you run npm for installing and saving modules.

Check your package.json file; it should say "main": "server.js".

The name of the file corresponds to what you entered during setup. Create a file called server.js in the root of your application (Listing 4-1).

Listing 4-1. server.js

```
1.   'use strict';
2.   const Hapi = require('hapi');
3.   const server = Hapi.server({
     port: 3000,
     host: 'localhost'
4.   });
5.   const init = async () =>
6.   {
7.       await server.start();
8.       console.log('Server running on %s', server.info.uri);
9.       server.route({
```

```
10.        method:'GET',
11.        path:'/home',
12.        handler: (request, h) => {
        return '<h3>Hello Kanika!</h3>';}});
13.
14.
15.    server.route({
16.            method:'GET',
17.            path:'/home/{name}',
18.            handler: (request, h) => {
19.            return `Hello ${request.params.name}!`;}});
20.
21.    process.on('unhandledRejection', (err) => {
22.    console.log(err);
23.    process.exit(1);
24.    });
25.    }; init();
```

On the first line, there are three things you need to know about the keyword **strict:**

- The purpose of use strict is to indicate that the code should be executed in "strict mode."

- With strict mode, you cannot, for example, use undeclared variables.

- All modern browsers support "use strict" except Internet Explorer 9 and lower.

We revisit the concept of loading dependencies at the end of the chapter; for now, just know that the require keyword is used to load a dependency onto hapi:

```
const Hapi = require('hapi');
```

A dependency in any framework is a library or a set of functions that can club execution. For "hapi," we're talking about the core hapi framework files that allow access to hapi modules, which in turn make programming in Node.js a whole lot of fun.

Now create the server with the following code:

```
const server = Hapi.server({
    port: 3000,
    host: 'localhost'
  });
```

The Server Object

The server object is the main application container. The object constructor has a host of options, the details of which can be read through the API docs at https://hapi.dev/ api/?v=18.4.0#-serveroptions.

For a good exercise in displaying what is accessible in the server.options offering, try the following code:

```
console.log('What does server have to offer?');
    for (let [key, value] of Object.entries(server)) {
        console.log(`${key}: ${value}`);
      }
```

The output for the server object is shown in Figure 4-5.

```
PROBLEMS  19    OUTPUT    DEBUG CONSOLE    TERMINAL

[nodemon] restarting due to changes...
[nodemon] starting `node .\server.js`
8000
server running at: http://LAPTOP-9IO63G1B:8000
What does server have to offer?
_core: [object Object]
app: [object Object]
auth: [object Object]
decorations: [object Object]
cache: function (options, _segment) {


        return this._core._cachePolicy(options, _segment, plugin.realm);
    }
events: [object Object]
info: [object Object]
listener: [object Object]
load: [object Object]
methods: [object Object]
mime: [object Object]
plugins: [object Object]
registrations: [object Object]
settings: [object Object]
states: [object Object]
type: tcp
version: 19.1.1
realm: [object Object]
Executing (default): SELECT 1+1 AS result
Database connection established.
```

Figure 4-5. *Console Output*

On line 8, we simply dump the server uri to the console:

```
console.log('Server running on %s', server.info.uri);
```

We use the port and host option settings in the constructor – line 3. The line can be used to set the port to 3000 and the host to local host or to whatever you wish.

The debug option should be explored:

```
server.options.debug
https://hapi.dev/api/?v=18.4.0#-serveroptionsdebug
```

We strongly recommend that you go through the API docs for more properties and methods on the server object. After you have taken a first look, proceed further to understanding the init method.

Benefits of the Optional Configuration Object

Compare the code in Listings 4-2 and 4-3 in any language.

Listing 4-2. Setting Configuration Through Class Methods

```
const app

const info = new server.info();

info.setPath('/kanika');
info.setPort('80');
```

Listing 4-3. Passing an Options Object

```
const options = {
    path: '/kanika',
    port: '80',
};

const app = new AnotherClass.options(options);
```

Listing 4-2 gives a more flexible way of passing an object. That is also the way you can pass an options object to the server constructor.

The Init Method

Line 5 of Listing 4-1 is where the action happens:

```
const init = async () =>
```

Notice that it's async. Basically, that means that this function can initiate a process, which can complete later on. Like the server.start() method, it has the keyword await for the same purpose. Read Chapter 3 for more information on **async** and **await**.

Adding Routes

If you followed our advice, you went through the hapi API docs, and if you did, you know how the route method is used. Here is a revisit:

```
server.route({
    method: 'GET',
    path: '/',
    handler: (request, h) => {
        return 'Hello World!';
    }
});
```

You're saying

1. Start a route.

2. Use an HTTP method (in this case GET).

3. Keep the path to the base path of the app. The path can contain parameters, which is discussed later in the sections that follow.

4. Define the handler (required when the handler is not set). The route handler is function called to generate the response after successful authentication and validation must return a value or a promise or throw an error.

Route Handling Internally

Routes in hapi are handled by a data structure called routing table. hapi's router will categorize each new route and add it to this data structure, and no matter which order you add your routes, the same routing table will be constructed. This is a huge plus vs. Express, where routing is first come, first serve.

Path Parameters in Routes

In our server.js file (Listing 4-1), see line 17:

```
15.  server.route({
16.          method:'GET',
17.          path:'/home/{name}',
18.          handler: (request, h) => {
19.          return `Hello ${request.params.name}!`;}});
```

On line 17, we add {name} to the path – what are we saying here? We are using path parameters. Whatever you provide as a path parameter to the path in the URL, we return the same param in the handler. While returning, we use the request object for accessing the query parameters and narrow down to name (as passed).

Handlers in Config

We personally find this method very useful, and hence we mention it here. This gives us the benefit of keeping all the configs together and then adding it to routes. Neat:

```
const user = {
    handler: function (request, h) {
        return { name: 'Kanika' };
    }
};

server.route({ method: 'GET', path: '/user', config: user });
```

The Process Object in Node.js

The process object is a global that provides information about, and control over, the current Node.js process. As a global, it is always available to Node.js applications without using require(). The process object is an instance of EventEmitter, which in turn is exposed by the events module. In our code, we use it for any unhandled rejections of the process object:

```
process.on('unhandledRejection', (err) => {
console.log(err);
process.exit(1);
});
```

Calling `init()` at the end of the file ensures that our server starts. To really understand what process object does in conjunction with the event loop, we recommend this site:

```
https://nodejs.dev/the-nodejs-event-loop
https://nodejs.dev/understanding-process-nexttick
```

Even though an insight into these can greatly enhance your understanding of Node.js and the call stack, we're skipping the details here, because we want you to know the practical aspects to getting an app up and running. Conceptually, just remember that any JavaScript code that takes too long to return back control to the event loop will block the execution. Even browsers rely on separate event loops for all tabs so that heavy processing in one tab doesn't block the browser. When programming, it's important not to make blocking calls like I/O or network calls synchronously; otherwise, being a single-threaded programming language, that one thread will occupy an indefinitely long time.

In fact, note how `process.nexttick()` can be used to tell how to bypass the queue and make any execution asynchronous.

Knowing how to set up our application and initialize our server is best tied with the knowledge of what package.json does. So we move on to the next component of our application: packages.

Component 2: Packages

A file that you must look at is `package.json`. It's at the root of the application when you generate a node app.

Here are the contents:

```
{
  "name": "hapi-starter",
  "version": "1.0.0",
  "description": "Starter App",
  "main": "server.js",
  "scripts": {
    "test": "echo \"Error: no test specified\" && exit 1"
  },
  "author": "",
  "license": "ISC",
```

```
  "dependencies": {
    "@hapi/hapi": "^19.0.5"
  }
}
```

What requires your attention here is

```
"main": "server.js"
```

and

```
"dependencies": {
    "@hapi/hapi": "^19.0.5"
  }
```

If these two are changed, your app fails, as the first sets the entry point to the app and the second sets the dependencies. Remember installing hapi.js? Installing dependencies on the command line is what adds them here. There is one tiny but important link to the package story in Node.js in version 5. And that is a file called package-lock.json, which we discuss next.

Package-lock.json

There is an automatically generated file which we showed in Figure 4-4. The file is called package-lock.json. What's it about? Well, it's a lot to do with module versioning.

The package-lock.json sets your currently installed version of each package, and npm will use those exact versions when running npm install whenever the project is being initialized with npm install.

Role of the Event Loop in Loading Dependencies

Since this topic is pertinent to all of Node.js irrespective of the framework, we visit it at the end of this chapter. Here we go.

When a node application begins, it registers dependencies and callbacks and plugins. The require keyword does that for you. Node applications then enter the event loop, responding to incoming client requests by executing the appropriate callbacks and loading a dependency as registered. On and off, we walk you through some of those phases when we develop full-blown applications later in the second half of the book.

Summary

The chapter walked us through a simple hapi app. We installed Node.js through the CLI, and we installed hapi.js through npm (which by the way, as most modern developers know, is a package manager for Node). We saw how installation at the command line altered our folder structure. We took a look at package.json, which told us two major things – the main entry point and a list of dependencies along with the versions of those dependencies. We described in detail the server.js file, for setting up a simple hapi.js app along the lines of a RESTful API, using a simple GET method and a path, adding parameters and a handler to its response.

In the next chapter, we'll explore our first REST API with hapi and MySQL.

CHAPTER 5

Building on the Basics: Validation, Authentication, and Plugins

In the previous chapter, we were able to show you how to get your first tiny app up and running. Now, we'll add the topping to the pizza. Before we dive into validating our requests, we organize them. After organizing our code, we validate our input using a library called Joi (pronounced joy), authenticate our routes, and build a minimal plugin to appreciate modularized code.

Note that we haven't added exception handling to any of our code, and that's intentional for now. We'll fill that gap in the next chapters as it's very easy to follow. As a standard, unhandled promise rejections are not good code practice.

Organizing Routes

Let's start with the code head-on. Later, we look at it, bit by bit. As before, initialize Node in a folder of your choice and fill out the details for the **package.json** file:

```
npm init

npm install @hapi/hapi --save
```

© Kanika Sud 2020
K. Sud, *Practical hapi*, https://doi.org/10.1007/978-1-4842-5805-7_5

In earlier versions of hapi, `npm install hapi --save` would work. Now, you'd need the preceding command because the package has been moved. (It happens, from time to time.) npm gives descriptive errors and warnings, provided you don't get intimidated by the console's way of putting it out on the stack. Should you get a warning or an error in the writing or execution of any code, do take the time to inspect the error – always a good practice.

Here's the **server.js** file:

```
1.   'use strict';
2.   const Hapi = require('hapi');
3.   const { configureRoutes } = require('./routes');
4.   const server = Hapi.server({
5.   port: 3000,
6.   host: 'localhost'
7.   });
8.   const init = async () =>
9.   {
     await server.start();
     await configureRoutes(server);
     console.log('Server running on %s',server.info.uri);
     process.on('unhandledRejection', (err) => {
     console.log(err);
     process.exit(1);
     });
10.  }; init();
```

Now create a folder called routes with an **index.js** file:

```
1.   'use strict';
2.   const Joi = require('joi');
3.   //configureroutes will be used in the main server.js file //to get the
     corresponding server.js file.
4.   exports.configureRoutes = (server) =>{
5.   return server.route([
```

```
6.    {
7.    method:'GET',
8.    path:'/home/{name}',
9.    handler: (request, h) => {
10.   return `Hello ${request.params.name}!`;} } }
```

If you get the following code running on the terminal, it means the app is running like before:

```
>node server.js
```

What have we done differently? We've organized all routes in a separate folder and loaded that in our server.js file.

Notice the **exports** keyword. The keyword should be familiar to developers of Node.js. For the ones who don't know about it, we're here to help. When you create a function that needs to be included externally outside of the file, you export it. The syntax is `exports.methodName = (parameters) => {}`.

It is because of the preceding line that you can use the method `configureroutes` in the server.js file, line 3.

Multiple Route Files   Note that in larger applications, routes are organized in multiple apps. We take that up in the next chapter.

We now speak of validating routes.

Validation

We added routes, but what if we want our services to check the kind of parameters that are passed? In our restaurant order analogy, you are limiting the kind of orders that are being placed on the counter:

```
npm install --save @hapi/joi
```

That command installs one of the best recommended libraries for validations.
Check the complete documentation here:

```
https://github.com/hapijs/joi
```

Our **routes/index.js** file changes a bit:

```
1.   'use strict';
2.   const Joi = require('@hapi/joi');
3.   //configure routes will be used in the main server.js file
     //to get the corresponding server.js file.
4.   exports.configureRoutes = (server) =>{
5.   return server.route([
6.   {
         method:'GET',
         path:'/home/{name}',
         handler: (request, h) => {
         return `Hello ${request.params.name}!`;}
7.   },
8.   {
         method:'POST',
         path:'/home/date/required',
         config: {
             validate: {
                 payload: joi.object({ date:Joi.date().required()
                 })
             }
         },
         handler: (request, h) => {
         return request.payload;}
     },
9.   {
         method:'POST',
         path:'/home/create/travel',
         config: {
             validate: {
                 payload: joi.object({ from :Joi.date().min('now').
                 required(),
                 to:Joi.date().greater(Joi.ref('from')).
                 required()})
                 }},
```

```
handler: (request, h) => {
return request.payload;
}
}]);}
```

We've added two request blocks: one on line 8 and one on line 9. And in both blocks, we demonstrate validation of dates, in a simple minimal manner.

const Joi = require('@hapijoi');

The preceding code loads the dependency for Joi (pronounced joy).

The following block validates anything that is given to the request (the data normally sent by a POST or PUT request):

```
config: {
  validate: {
  payload: joi.object({ date: Joi.date().required()})
  }}
```

date: Joi.date().required() tells the server that the request expects a parameter called **date** and it is required. It also validates as per the validation rules of the **Joi.date()** function.

Open a REST API client, like POSTMAN, and run the server and hit the request, and you should see the screen shown in Figure 5-1.

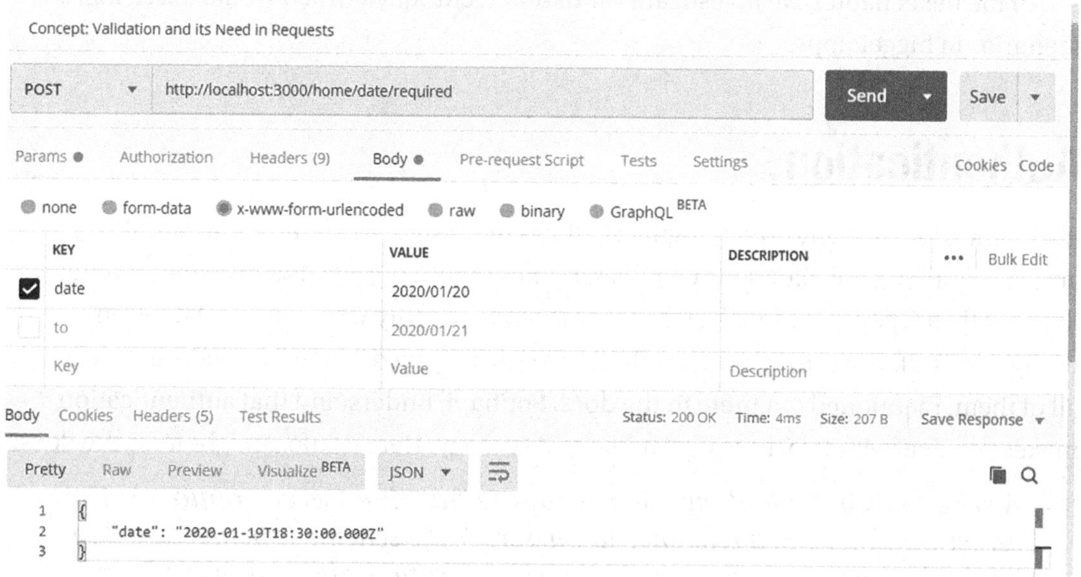

Figure 5-1. *Output from Validating the Date with Joi*

Try changing the name of the parameter to, say, "whatdate"; and it sends an error:

```
{
    "statusCode": 400,
    "error": "Bad Request",
    "message": "Invalid request payload input"
}
```

Try changing the value of the parameter date to something which isn't a date, say, a normal string **jsdhk;** and it sends an error. The following is the second request block in our code on line number 9:

```
config: {
validate: {
payload: joi.object({
from :Joi.date().min('now').required(),
to:Joi.date().greater(Joi.ref('from')).required( )
})
}},
```

This shows how Joi allows you to set a minimum value of the date and how another date should be greater than the first. `Joi.ref()` allows you to refer to another payload field in the same block.

In the next chapter, we investigate validation techniques which would serve more scenarios in bigger apps.

Authentication

Authentication, like any other language, allows the system to identify who should access a system. hapi allows for various schemes (check out the documentation here: `https://hapi.dev/plugins/#authentication`) to identify who you are. And even though we walk you through two methods, we strongly recommend you take a shot at all of them, mentioned out there in the docs. For hapi, understand that authentication makes you deal with two things – scheme and strategy. Here is info straight from the docs:

*A **scheme** is a method with the signature function (server, options). The server parameter is a reference to the server the scheme is being added to, while the options parameter is the configuration object provided when* *registering a strategy that uses this scheme. This method must return an object with at least the key **authenticate**. Other optional methods that can be used are **payload** and **response**.*

Basic Auth

https://hapi.dev/family/basic/api/?v=6.0.0

The docs provide a fairly good idea of how the basic auth can be used. For those of us who don't know what basic auth is, it provides for a simple username-password mechanism of logging in. Again, we have an example straight from the docs:

```
//server.js
1.   'use strict';

2.   const Hapi = require('@hapi/hapi');

3.   const users = {
john: {
username: 'john',
password: 'pass1',
name: 'John Doe',
id: '2133d32a'
}
};

4.   const validate = async (request, username, password) => {
const user = users[username];
if (!user) {
return { credentials: null, isValid: false };
}

const isValid = (password === user.password)?true:false;
const credentials = { id: user.id, name: user.name };

return { isValid, credentials };
};
```

```
5.    const start = async () => {

const server = Hapi.server({ port: 4000 });

await server.register(require('@hapi/basic'));

server.auth.strategy('simple', 'basic', { validate });

server.route({
method: 'GET',
path: '/',
options: {
auth: 'simple'
},
handler: function (request, h) {
    console.log(h);
  return request.auth.credentials; }
});

await server.start();

console.log('server running at: ' + server.info.uri);
};

6.    start();
```

Use this code for a single-file application. And test the API in POSTMAN. Here's what you get when you key in the parameters for logging into the Authorization tab. Select Basic from the Authorization tab:

1. For the wrong username or password, the response is helpful:

```
{
    "statusCode": 401,
    "error": "Unauthorized",
    "message": "Bad username or password",
    "attributes": {
        "error": "Bad username or password"
    }
}
```

2. For the right credentials, we return the credentials object
    (explained in detail later):

```
request.auth.credentials;
```

As an exercise, try adding the basic auth to the validation app as well. The solution
code is provided in the source code folders.

Understanding the Code

The following line registers the basic auth plugin for hapi:

```
await server.register(require('@hapi/basic'));
```

This line registers the basic scheme for the app authentication. Scheme here means
the scheme offered by hapi, for authentication and the one which just registered in
the line above. The scheme definition that we were talking about is defined inside this
plugin, and server.auth.scheme() inside the plugin code takes care of it. On line
number 5, the start() function shows you how to register the plugin here, followed by
stating the strategy:

```
server.auth.strategy('simple', 'basic', { validate });
```

When you refer to the basic scheme in your code, you'll do so by using the first
identifier simple. The second is the scheme that we just registered in the preceding
text. The third argument to the function is the function validate. It is required. It
always helps to check the full signature of a function and for the server.auth.strategy
function. Here it is:

```
function(request, username, password), where
```

request – The hapi request object which requires authentication
username – Username sent by the client
password – Password sent by the client
This is a required function which states how to validate your request.

We have included a console log of the response toolkit. Check it out for seeing very
useful options, including the h.auth object.

The way the validate function works is simple: within, we've created a user object by including the username provided by the user at the time of the request. If the username isn't an attribute in the use object, the user variable isn't constructed, and we return an invalid status. Else, we return the credentials object, which is available because of the validate function, passed through the `request.auth.options` config, a combination workflow of these lines:

```
options: {
    auth: 'simple'
}
  const credentials = { id: user.id, name: user.name };
```

Notice if you add another attribute to the credentials object, you can use it too:

```
const credentials = { id: user.id, name: user.name, username: user.
username };
```

The response would have then been

```
{
    "id": "2133d32a",
    "name": "John Doe",
    "username": "john"
}
```

This shows you that the credentials object is added to the auth attribute of the request object and is set when we code the validate function.

The validate function can return a fourth optional object response. This can be tailored for custom messages or redirects. Check the complete basic auth scheme here: `https://hapi.dev/family/basic/api/?v=6.0.0`

---

hapi-auth-jwt2

This is another plugin we recommend for authentication. We take up a detailed explanation in later chapters, but here we suggest you just clone a repository and see it's working:

```
git clone https://github.com/dwyl/hapi-auth-jwt2.git
```

Making a Plugin and module.exports

Let's put the authentication code inside a plugin.

Taken step by step, here is what we do:

```
>mkdir hapi-plugins
>cd hapi-plugins
>npm init
```

After creating a `package.json` file, create a file called `index.js` (name it whatever you used as an entry point in the package.json).

After installing your dependencies, `@hapi/hapi` and `@hapi/basic`, create a folder called auth and a file called index.js in it. Here's the code for auth/index.js:

```
// auth/index.js
var authPlugin = {

  register: function (server, options) {

    const users = {
        john: {
            username: 'john',
            password: 'pass1',
            name: 'John Doe',
            id: '2133d32a'
        }
    };

  module.exports.validate = async (request, username, password) => {

        const user = users[username];
        if (!user) {
            return { credentials: null, isValid: false };
        }

        var isValid = false;
        if(password === user.password)
        {
            isValid = true;
        }
```

```
        const credentials = { id: user.id, name: user.name, username: user.
        username };

        return { isValid, credentials };
    };
  },
  name: 'authPlugin'
}
```

module.exports = authPlugin

The line module.exports.validate is what makes the code a valid public accessible method:

```
var authPlugin = {

register: function (server, options) { … },
name: 'authPlugin'
}
```

This is what makes the code a plugin.

The entry point index.js changes from our authentication example before as in

```
'use strict';

const Hapi = require('@hapi/hapi');
//load the plugin files, similar to loading a dependency
const Auth = require('./auth');

const start = async () => {

const server = Hapi.server({ port: 8000 });

await server.register(require('@hapi/basic'));
//register the plugin with the identifier used above
await server.register({plugin:Auth});

//the simple strategy, basic scheme, and validate methods //passed - this
time with the Auth.validate identifier.
server.auth.strategy('simple', 'basic', { validate : Auth.validate });
```

```
server.route({
        method: 'GET',
        path: '/',
        options: {
            auth: 'simple'
        },
        handler: function (request, h) {
            console.log(h);
            return request.auth.credentials;
        }
    });

    await server.start();

    console.log('server running at: ' + server.info.uri);
};

start();
```

This is what has changed:

//load the plugin files, similar to loading a dependency
```
const Auth = require('./auth');
```

//register the plugin with the identifier used above
```
await server.register({plugin:Auth});
```

//the simple strategy, basic scheme, and validate methods //passed - this time with the Auth.validate identifier.
```
server.auth.strategy('simple', 'basic', { validate : Auth.validate });
```

Let's run it:

```
>npm install @hapi/hapi --save
>npm install @hapi/basic --save
```

On POSTMAN, the following URL with the same authorization headers as before, and authentication method as basic, will yield an identical response:

```
http://localhost:8000/
```

```
{
    "id": "2133d32a",
    "name": "John Doe",
    "username": "john"
}
```

Summary

This chapter enabled you to make your simple hapi app more holistic. Since no app would exist without authentication and validation and plugins are going to be used in any huge application, we thought this was the right time in this book to introduce you to these concepts. We've purposefully left out database connectivity as understanding it with our capstone project would make it for holistic learning.

Further Reading

Developer docs on hapi authentication – `https://hapi.dev/tutorials/auth/?lang=en_US`

A good intro to the plugin – `https://hapi.dev/family/basic/api/?v=6.0.0#usage`

The place to go for understanding strategies in authentication – `https://hapi.dev/api/?v=19.0.5#-serverauthstrategyname-scheme-options`

CHAPTER 6

Database Connectivity

In the previous chapter, we climbed a ladder to the next level of hapi apps. We spiced the app with validations, plugins, and authentication. Here, we use the toppings, along with database connectivity, to make the skeleton for an industry-ready RESTful Web Service. Apart from our main topic of database connectivity, we find it important to introduce a few development utilities at this juncture, so that we can improve our development journey.

For a reference, or revisit, you should now be able to

- Initialize Node and create the app skeleton – Chapter 4.

- Make plugins – Chapter 5.

- Validate – Chapter 5.

- Authenticate – Chapter 5.

- Remove all your doubts about REST – Chapter 1.

Databases

Databases are helpful for adding persistence to an application. Most industry applications would be incomplete without data-driven business logic. Even though MongoDB is a commonly considered choice with Node.js applications, we prefer to stick with MySQL unless the nature of your application demands document-based storage. The Appendix makes a short remark on what document-based storage is. We also encourage you to read about the pros and cons of different types of database systems and different database dialects before using a database for your own personal application, as the choice of technology might be considered a scope larger than that of this book.

© Kanika Sud 2020

K. Sud, *Practical hapi*, https://doi.org/10.1007/978-1-4842-5805-7_6

You're ultimately out there for data. And since ORMs (search the Internet if you're not familiar) are the best way to model relational databases in apps, let's choose our ORM and get on with work. If you look through the Internet, you'll find that Sequelize comes in as a handy choice for Node.js ORMs, and one of the main reasons is the continuous support for many dialects: Postgres, MySQL, MariaDB, SQLite, and Microsoft SQL Server. Some very useful features that might fast-track your development cycle include but are not limited to the following:

1. A well-managed Associations API is a criterion to investigate any ORM when considering your choices – simply because all your tables in a relational database will be mapped to each other.

2. What if you wish to migrate a schema? Does your ORM allow for it?

3. Validation of data is very essential in both APIs and web apps, but more so in APIs, because the APIs are completely independent of client-side validation. Where and in which manner your API might be used, you might not know at the time of writing it, and so validating data while storing it to the database is a good criterion.

4. In data-intensive applications, with a lot of risk, transaction-oriented operations on the database are necessary. Managing transactions, through well-organized commit and rollback, is important in an ORM. Before you choose one, and when you're learning an ORM, this might be a good thing to grasp.

5. Any features apart from this, such as multi-server handling and lazy loading, are extra pluses of a good ORM.

Using Sequelize

While using Sequelize, we mainly cover connecting to the database and Sequelize configuration in the following subsections. We also cover distributed models in different files, which explains how to parameterize an import across various files into one. From here on, the main aim is to familiarize you with database setup for a data-driven app.

Check the complete documentation here:

```
https://sequelize.org/v5/index.html
```

If you go through the features in the preceding link and compare them with the criteria we gave, you'll understand why Sequelize is a better choice for apps demanding modeling of databases.

Connecting to the Database

Let's make a small app to demonstrate connectors. The app after this will show interconnected routed files for the database and how to store information in the database. We then proceed to register and log into the app, using our model. After a basic CRUD functionality with the database is created, we end the chapter with a summary on database tools, best practices, and next steps of using the same code in our capstone project.

For our next app, here's the folder structure, after making the skeleton of the app under the root:

```
dbConfig/index.js
node_modules/
package.json
server.js
```

Install mysql2 and sequelize as dependencies.

We expect by now we won't have to reiterate the steps to make a preliminary hapi app. You can always refer back to the chapters for reference, as cited in the preceding text.

Here's the code for the server.js file:

```
//server.js
'use strict';

const Hapi = require('@hapi/hapi');
const Connection = require('./dbConfig');
```

```
const start = async () => {

    const server = Hapi.server({ port: 8000 });

    await server.start();

    console.log('server running at: ' + server.info.uri);
};

start();
```

Here's the code for the package.json file (versions of node modules will differ; just note the ones we have here):

```
{
  "name": "hapi-database",
  "version": "1.0.0",
  "description": "Simple Connection to the Database",
  "main": "server.js",
  "scripts": {
    "test": "echo \"Error: no test specified\" && exit 1"
  },
  "author": "Kanika Sud",
  "license": "ISC",
  "dependencies": {
    "@hapi/basic": "^6.0.0",
    "@hapi/hapi": "^19.0.5",
    "mysql2": "^2.1.0",
    "sequelize": "^5.21.3"
  }
}
```

Inside the folder dbConfig, make a file called index.js:

1.    ```
      const Sequelize = require('sequelize');
      ```

2.    ```
      const seq = new Sequelize('pollme', 'root', 'admin', {
      host: 'localhost',
      port:'3306',
      dialect: 'mysql'
      });
      ```

```
3.   seq.authenticate().then(
4.   ()=>{console.log("Database connection established.");} )
5.   .catch(err=>
        { console.error('Connection Disrupted.', err);});
```

Ensure that the MYSQL service is running on the local host and run the node app. The following is the expected output:

```
server running at: http://LAPTOP-9I063G1B:8000
Executing (default): SELECT 1+1 AS result
Database connection established.
```

Sequelize Configuration

Line by line, we take up the small file that did the database wonder:

```
1.   const Sequelize = require('sequelize');
```

We're basically importing the module sequelize and making its functions available to our code:

```
2.   const seq = new Sequelize('pollme', 'root', 'admin',
     {
     host: 'localhost',
     port:'3306',
     dialect: 'mysql'
     });
```

We made an instance of Sequelize and specified our database name, username, and password for it.

The fourth parameter is the options object, to which we pass the host, port, dialect.

Notice that our dependency of mysql2 installed in the beginning (refer to package.json) is reflected by the dialect we use in Sequelize.

This instance is handy whenever we want to mention our connection object elsewhere in code – like when we authenticate and log into the database or pass instances to model definitions.

```
3.   seq.authenticate().then(
     ()=>{console.log("Database connection established.");}
```

67

If all's well, your database connection is successfully established; else, you catch the error and throw it.

That's all you got to do!

In the next section, we explore some important tools that fast-track development.

Handy Tools, Utilities, and Practices

Your tools determine how smooth your journey will be. Let's take a short detour to tools and extras. Up till now, we have discussed details of code. But you might have noticed a few hiccups:

- Whenever you make changes in a Node.js app, you'd need to restart the server for the changes to reflect.

    - Solution – `nodemon`. This is taken up in this section.

- We haven't discussed any utility that could help in syntax highlighting, IntelliSense, and the like. No IDE was taken up, and this could hamper your journey further.

    - Solution – For a simpler app, you could go for Visual Studio Code and its extensions. Install **Visual Studio Code** and search the marketplace for suitable extensions. Practice is what keeps your hang on it. If you are choosing to stick with Node.js for a longer run, **IntelliJ IDEA** could be a good solution. Here too, you need a Node.js plugin to enable the features, including syntax highlighting, code assistance, code completion, and more. You can run and debug Node.js apps and see the results right in the IDE. Its JavaScript debugger offers conditional breakpoints, expression evaluation, and other features. If you're a good old Eclipse fan, like I am, even though it's an overkill for smaller apps, go with Eclipse and the **Enide plugin** from the Eclipse marketplace. Steps to getting your IDE comfort: play, experiment, fail, and succeed!

- You've limited yourself to console logs. We haven't introduced logging. We haven't looked at common errors in Node.js. Speaking of which, how about debugging an app through the tools we use? Yeah, always a good idea.

  - Solution – `good,` a package suitable for logging. This is discussed in the next chapter. There are built-in methods too, and we will take them up in brief as well.

- You've not followed packaging an app on a larger scale. For Node. js, it can be quite a headache. And sometimes, the way your app is packaged can be quite a difficult situation in code. There are plenty of ways available, and choosing one may be difficult.

  - Solution – The way we do it, we choose one way, as will be explained in this section; stick to it, and explain the benefits of it.

- We haven't discussed industry practices like generating API documentation.

  - We'll discuss `Swagger` soon, along with its configuration details for hapi.

nodemon

The official documentation (`www.npmjs.com/package/nodemon`) states

> *nodemon is a tool that helps develop node.js based applications by automatically restarting the node application when file changes in the directory are detected.*

Now, the reason we introduce it here is that we are going to take up a bigger app and build it iteratively – so it's always a good idea to refresh the request, rather than restart the server for every small change. If you need to manually restart your application, instead of stopping and restarting nodemon, you can type `rs` with a carriage return, and nodemon will restart your process.

Here are the steps:

```
npm install -g nodemon
```

That's it – and nodemon will be installed globally to your system path. Installing it globally is better than adding it as a dependency, as the benefit applies to all node projects, not just one. On a local installation, you'd have to run it from an npm script (not discussed here).

To demonstrate our point, take the previous example – "hapi-database". Keep the same source code, and after having installed the nodemon utility, run the app. Thus:

```
D:\hapijs\ApressBook\hapi-database>nodemon server.js
```

While it's still running, change the code. For instance, change the server.js file and add an app.settings option.

Your server.js file now looks like

```
'use strict';
const Hapi = require('@hapi/hapi');
const Connection = require('./dbConfig');

const start = async () => {

const server = Hapi.server({ port: 8000, app: {app_name:'hapi_database'}
}); //Modified to demo Nodemon.

    await server.start();
console.log('server running at: ' + server.info.uri);
console.log('*App Name: ' + server.settings.app.app_name); //Added to demo
Nodemon.
};

start();
```

You'll notice that the process doesn't require you to exit and restart as it did before. For example, if you do the preceding exercise, with node server.js instead of nodemon server.js, you'd still have to exit and manually restart.

Models and App Workflow

Introducing Models into Your App

Look at the source code of the app: "hapi-database-orm-full." Figure 6-1 shows the folder structure.

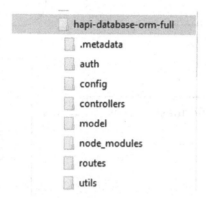

Figure 6-1. *The Folder Structure for an App with Models, Controllers, and Utilities*

At the root level, you have your usual file of package.json, server.js. So what we've done is we've created three layers:

- model
- utils
- controllers

Moreover, routes add to the chain and select the suitable path, as shown schematically in Figure 6-2.

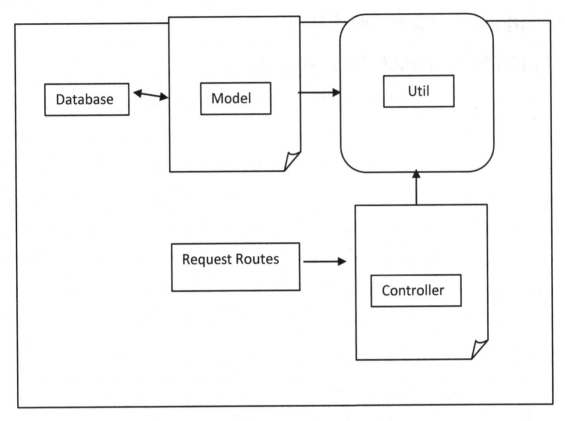

Figure 6-2. *Structuring an MVC App*

This is common practice in any MVC framework in any language. Now, what we do in our hapi app is that we add an index file to each folder and sub-files representing the roles of that folder. For example, Figures 6-3 through 6-5 show the model layer structure.

> hapijs > ApressBook > hapi-database-orm-full > model

Name	Date modified
index	15-02-2020 08:47
User	15-02-2020 08:59

Figure 6-3. *The model Folder*

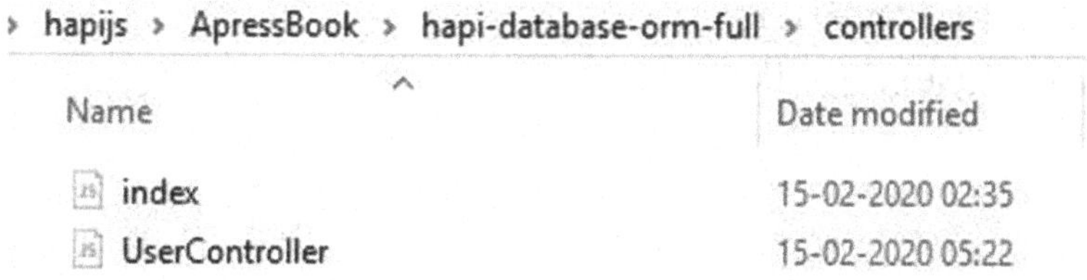

Figure 6-4. *The controllers Folder*

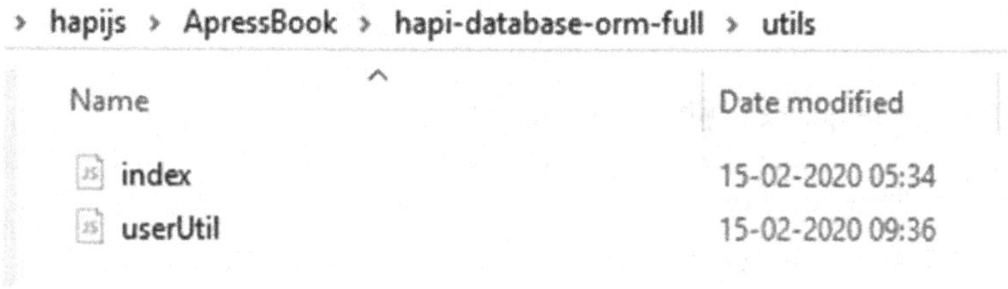

Figure 6-5. *The utils Folder*

Let's add some preliminary code to all these files and understand the flow better. After you have created the preceding folder structure and a skeletal app with npm init, load the dependencies in the order required and fill in the following in the files mentioned below.

The file server.js defines the routes that are used in this app. These routes are then exported to the index.js file of the same folder. Listings 6-1 and 6-2 explain the exporting of routes.

Listing 6-1. routes/index.js

```
//routes/index.js
//
// //
//the idea is to keep routes specific to the user, in one //file.
//and when the application expands, we can have routes related //to polls
in another file. All will be exported to index.js
module.exports = [
    {
        method: 'GET',
        path: '/getUsers',
        handler: function (request, h) {
```

```
        console.log("getUsers");
        return  {user:"Kanika"};
   }
}];
```

Listing 6-2.   Server.js

//Server.js to reflect the changes in routing
```
'use strict';
```

```
1.    const hapi = require('@hapi/hapi');
2.    const routes = require('./routes');
```

```
3.    const start = async () => {
      const server = hapi.server({ port: 3000 });
      server.route(routes); //routes imported on top, line 2.

      await server.start();
      console.log('server running at: ' + server.info.uri);
```
      //Print Order On Console - 1
```
4.    };
5.    start();
```

If you run the preceding app, you'll notice that the routes are imported perfectly:

```
http://localhost:3000/getUsers
```

would give: `{"user":"Kanika"}`

The Workflow

```
server.route(routes);
```

This line used the `routes` object and added it to the `server.routes`:

```
const routes = require('./routes');
```

This module "./routes/index" was imported by line number 1, which provided for

```
module.exports = [
    {
        method: 'GET',
        path: '/getUsers',
        handler: function (request, h) {
        console.log("getUsers");  return  {user:"Kanika"};      }
}];
```

Read it as follows: Look for the routes object, if defined or imported, get routes and its exports (or definition), and add it to the **server.route** method.

Now, add a folder called config at the root level. Add files called appConfig.js and dbConifg.js (Listings 6-3 through 6-5).

Such configs are very useful for values that will differ according to environments, or choosing an environment itself, application messages, internationalization, and so on. While many use the dotenv utility, we prefer to go the app constants way. We slightly touched on a method of adding an option in the server constructor and retrieving it by `server.settings.variable_name.` That can come in handy for the application name and domain name that will remain the same.

Listing 6-3. appConfig.js

```
//appConfig.js
var APP_CONSTANTS = {
  DEVELOPMENT:
  {
    APP_PORT:8000
  },
  PRODUCTION:
  {
    APP_PORT:3000
  }
};

module.exports = APP_CONSTANTS;
```

Listing 6-4. dbConfig.js

//dbConfig.js

```
var DB_CONSTANTS = {
    DEVELOPMENT:
    {
      DB_PORT: 3306,
      DIALECT: 'mysql',
      DB_NAME:'pollme',
      DB_PASS:'admin',
      DB_USER:'root',
      DB_HOST:'localhost',
    },
    PRODUCTION:
    {
        DB_PORT: 3306,
        DIALECT: 'mysql'
    }
};

module.exports = DB_CONSTANTS;
```

Listing 6-5. config/index.js

//config/index.js
```
const appConfig = require('./appConfig');
const dbConfig = require('./dbConfig');

module.exports =
  {
    appConfig:appConfig,
    dbConfig:dbConfig
  }
```

Now, revisit your file `server.js` (check Listing 6-2), and on line number 3, replace the existing content with

```
const server = hapi.server({ port: config.appConfig.DEVELOPMENT.APP_PORT
});
```

Listing 6-6 is the final server.js.

Listing 6-6. server.js After All Modifications

```
'use strict';
const config = require('./config'); //import config/index.js
const hapi = require('@hapi/hapi');
const routes = require('./routes');
const start = async () => {

    const server = hapi.server({ port: config.appConfig.DEVELOPMENT.APP_
    PORT });
    //check definition or exports

    server.route(routes);
    await server.start();
    console.log('server running at: ' + server.info.uri);
};
start();
```

This produces the same output as before (Figure 6-6).

```
[nodemon] clean exit - waiting for changes before restart
[nodemon] restarting due to changes...
[nodemon] starting `node .\server.js`
server running at: http://LAPTOP-9IO63G1B:8000
```

Figure 6-6. *server.js.output*

And on http://localhost:3000/getUsers:

```
{"user":"Kanika"}
```

The config object has an imported appConfig which has an imported DEVELOPMENT object:

```
config.appConfig.DEVELOPMENT.APP_PORT
```

Whenever you load a dependency through a folder, everything exported through the index.js file is exported.

We used the same strategy when we created a plugin. As an exercise, before going ahead, try creating the auth folder on your own, import it in the server.js file, and add the authentication scheme through the object imported. Registering a plugin is done, as explained earlier. With `Sequelize` models, this is a little trickier, because the connection or `sequelize` object exported needs to be of the same type; and therefore, while exporting, we need to pass the types as parameters. Even if this sounds Greek, take it – we'll make it simple in a moment.

In your model folder, add the code from Listings 6-7 and 6-8.

Listing 6-7. Index File of the model Folder

```
//model/index.js
const sequelize = require('sequelize');
const config = require('../config');

const connection = new sequelize(config.dbConfig.DEVELOPMENT.DB_NAME,
    config.dbConfig.DEVELOPMENT.DB_USER,
    config.dbConfig.DEVELOPMENT.DB_PASS,
    {
      host: config.dbConfig.DEVELOPMENT.DB_HOST,
      port: config.dbConfig.DEVELOPMENT.DB_PORT,
      dialect: config.dbConfig.DEVELOPMENT.DIALECT,
      pool: {
      max: 5,
      min: 0,
      idle: 10000
    }
    }
    );
```

```
connection.authenticate().then(
    ()=>{console.log("Database connection established.");}  //Print
    Order - 2
  ).catch(err=>
    {console.error('Connection Disrupted.', err);});

module.exports =
{
  usersModel:require('./User')(connection)
}
```

Listing 6-8. User Model Exported to the Index in the model Folder

//User.js
```
1.   const dataTypes = require('sequelize');
2.   var user;
3.   module.exports = function(connection){
4.   user = connection.define('User', {
5.   userid:
6.   {
         primaryKey: true,
         allowNull: false,
         type: dataTypes.INTEGER,
         autoIncrement: true
7.   },
8.   firstName: {
           type: dataTypes.STRING,
           unique: true,
           allowNull: false },
9.   lastName: {
           type: dataTypes.STRING,
           allowNull: false }
10.  },{ timestamps : false } )
11.  return user; };
```

Models in Different Files

Basically, you're trying to say that you'll place different models in different files, but how do you pass the same `sequelize` instance through and through, since everything works with exports? Answer:

```
usersModel:require('./User')(connection)
module.exports = function(connection)
```

This is a parameterized import, saying that the User.js model file can be exported through usersModel, and whenever it is used (exported) in the index.js file, you can use it with the same connection parameter. Note that you could also backtrack requiring index.js in the individual module files – that breaks a lot of general convention, and we don't adopt that approach. The idea is to make the connection instance available, so that it is defined once and used in every model:

Coming from a Java background, I found JavaScript hard to grasp at first, and when simple things like routing became complex, it seemed quite a deterrent. Having said that, lightweight frameworks, which have an easy learning curve, and an everything-in-JavaScript approach still keep me hooked to the language. If you're through with the flow, move on; if not, revisit the flow, play with it, and make sure you know it, before stepping onward.

```
const dataTypes = require('sequelize');
```

We define a const of type sequelize. When we use the static variables to represent data types, however, we use `dataTypes.INTEGER` and so on.

Now check lines 3 and 4 of the preceding code listing:

```
module.exports = function(connection){
user = connection.define('User', {
```

We pass in a connection instance to the function, and we use that to define the model name. The syntax is given in the following:

```
var = connectionInstance.define('ModelName', {attributes}, {options});
```

Notice that you need the connection *instance* and not the connection reference dataTypes when you define a model.

We will now put out our code for the controllers and utils, and for now, they do nothing but for navigation (Listings 6-9 through 6-11).

Listing 6-9. The User Util File in the Utility Layer

//utils\userUtil.js
```
const models = require('../model');

async function fetchUsers() {
    console.log("Inside utils::userUtil.js::fetchUsers");
    var listUsers = {};
    try{
    listUsers = await models.usersModel.findAll({
        attributes: ['firstName', 'lastName']
    })

    }catch(err)
    {
        console.error(err);
        throw err;
    }
    return {listUsers:listUsers};
    }
module.exports = {
    fetchUsers:fetchUsers
}
```

//utils\index.js
```
module.exports = {
    userUtil:require('./userUtil')
}
```

Listing 6-10. The Main Routes File

//routes/index.js
```
var controllers = require('../controllers');
module.exports = [
```

```
  {
  method: 'GET',
  path: '/',
  options: {
      auth: 'simple'
  },
  handler: function (request, h) {
      console.log(h);
      return request.auth.credentials;
  }},
  {
      method: 'GET',
      path: '/getUsers',
      handler: async function (request, h) {
          try
          {
          var allUsers = controllers.userController.fetchUsers();
              console.log("success");
              return allUsers;
          }catch(err)
          { throw err };

  }

}];
```

Listing 6-11. The User Controller File in The Controllers Layer

//controllers/userController.js
```
var utils = require('../utils');
async function fetchUsers() {
console.log("Inside controllers::userController.js::fetchUsers");
  var users = {}
  users = await utils.userUtil.fetchUsers().then(
          function(users)
```

```
        {
             return users;
        }).catch(err=>
        {console.error('Ouch', err);});

    return users;
}

module.exports =
{
  fetchUsers:fetchUsers
}
```

On POSTMAN, this would give you the following now:

```
{
    "listUsers": [
        {
             "firstName": "John",
             "lastName": "Hancock"
        }
    ]
}
```

or whatever data you do have in the DB.

Here are the things to try out:

- If you remove asynchronous programming from the model **User.js** and make it synchronous:

```
listUsers = await models.usersModel.findAll({
    attributes: ['firstName', 'lastName']
})
```

- Don't worry. We'll walk through these last trails in the Appendix. But give it a shot.

- What happens if you do not return from a handler in the route configuration?

Please note the following:

- Sequelize can very fairly fast-track your development process, especially if you get your hands on the querying mechanism. Check the docs for more.

- Sequelize can prevent what is called the SQL injection attacks, which would hugely affect an application.

- Exporting is an outward spiral – everything exported through the index.js file is exported to the file where it is imported (required).

Summary

This chapter enabled you to package an app and explore tools, with a brief touch on standard practices, ORM considerations, and Sequelize, a mention of Swagger for documentation, and a glimpse of how models are defined and queried. We learned how to follow a decent structure for our app, including models in different files (parameterized imports), and how all would have an impact on the final app in a single workflow. We have what it takes to make an app.

CHAPTER 7

Capstone Project: REST API for Polling App

We have, by far, made everything we need for a data-driven REST API. Even if we don't learn further, we will be able to make a rich REST API application, considering what we know about hapi and a little bit more research about Sequelize and other plugins we've used. The little loose ends, those things we call bugs, are included in the Appendix. So what's left now? Well, the book wasn't just about hapi, it was more about preparing you for the industry where hapi is catching up quickly. Preparing for the industry, if you're not already in it, includes a ground-up approach to understanding a use case. Let's get right into the show.

Product Storyline

We design a polling app, whereby authenticated users can create a poll, share it, and view a feed. Every step of the storyline either introduces a new concept or takes an already introduced concept to the next level – it's just that we add industry-level practices to it, right from password encryption to logging to testing. So our chapter flow is

- Designing a solution

- Designing a database

- Modeling the database (concept: validators and constraints)

- Registering a user (concept: understanding hooks, utilities for hashing passwords)

- Authenticating a user (concept: statelessness revisited, token bearer)

© Kanika Sud 2020

K. Sud, *Practical hapi*, https://doi.org/10.1007/978-1-4842-5805-7_7

- Creating poll associations (concept: understanding associations)

- Deleting associated objects (concept: cascade delete)

- Creating an optimized feed (concept: understanding raw queries, introducing logging)

Designing the Solution

The real crux of any engineering activity is in its design. If you spend more than 30% of the time in design and try to uncover as many problems as possible in its initial phases, you'll face no problems in its code. That's hardly the case, as the industry doesn't give you the privilege of time, but when making a product which allows for time, you should for sure spend more time on designing the solution and then proceed to code.

Polls

A poll, as we all know, is a form with a question and multiple-choice answers to it. You spread the poll question, among a given set of users. The users respond to the poll and answer the question, and we take an analysis of the users who voted for each poll option in a poll, the results stating the option that won the vote.

We made a mind map of the solution we have in mind (Figure 7-1). We have these main entities in our user story:

- Poll

- Poll Option

- Poll Result

- Poll Vote

- User

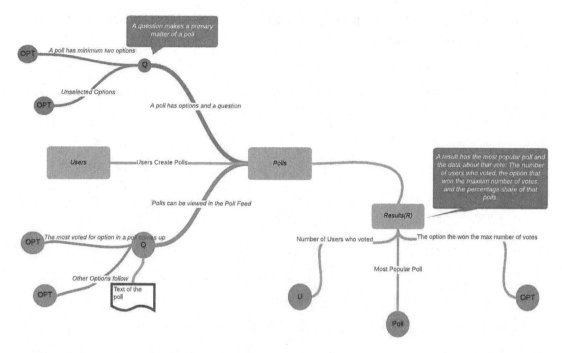

Figure 7-1. *Mind Map: Polling App*

As we go along, we can explain the story better.

We first begin by making a database. As already stated, we are making a database in MySQL, and here I give some recommendations for a GUI for MySQL:

- SQLyog – www.webyog.com/

- DBeaver – https://dbeaver.io/download/

We use the second. It has an awesome interface to connect to many kinds of SQL servers, not just MySQL – both remote and local. Adding constraints, foreign keys, references, and indexes from the GUI is all easy; and so we have no trouble in designing our database and presenting the ER diagram quickly.

Here are the basic ER diagrams (Figure 7-2) for our four tables (and trust us, for a solid grip, we need no more!):

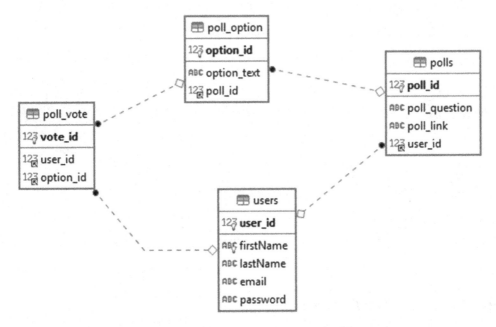

Figure 7-2. *Entity Relationship Between Our Major Tables*

So in terms of **IS A** and **HAS A** terminology

- A "Poll" has a "Users" object (users who created that poll) and a "Poll Option" object:

  - Relationship between Poll and Users – A one-to-one relationship exists between these two tables.

  - Relationship between Poll and Option – A one-to-many relationship exists between these two tables.

- A "Poll Vote" has a "Poll Option" object and a "Users" object:

  - Relationship between Poll Vote and Poll Option – One-to-one

  - Constraint

    - The mapping between user_id and option_id is unique in that a particular user is only allowed to choose a single option. Once you vote for an option, you can't vote for it again.

- Even though voting for multiple or single options should be ideally kept from the front end, you can if you wish opt for another constraint: the mapping between user_id and poll_id can be unique, that is, we allow the combination of a user_id and a poll_id only once in a table. This means the user can hit only one option for a poll, not two.

In our solution, we're choosing not to store the poll results in the database. Such results should be calculated dynamically.

Individually, the entities can be represented minimally as such in Figure 7-3 (more fields can be added later).

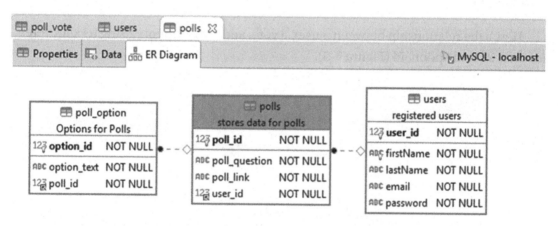

Figure 7-3. *Polls Table*

While designing a database, it's always a good idea to keep a check on its ER diagram. All good database GUIs give a good view, and we can thus check our entity relationships (Figure 7-4).

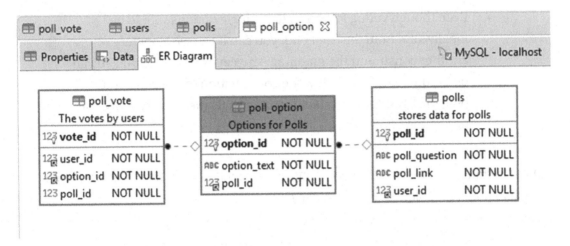

Figure 7-4. *ER Diagram Showing the Relationship Between vote_id, option_id, and poll_id*

Here's the relationship between a user, a vote, and a vote option, using its keys vote_id, user_id, and option_id (Figure 7-5).

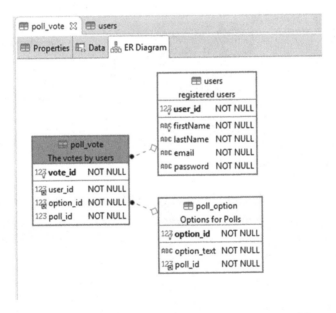

Figure 7-5. *Polls Vote Table and the Relationship Between a User, a Vote, and an Option*

Keep in mind that the story starts from the user table. Here is the ER diagram for it (Figure 7-6).

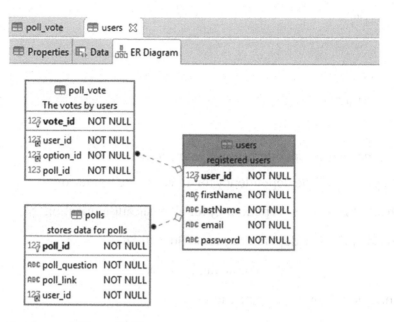

Figure 7-6. *Registered Users Table*

Beginning the Code

Start a project with the following package.json and the rest of the structure remaining the same as the application we made in the last chapter (Listing 7-1).

Listing 7-1. Package.json for Our Industry Project

```
//package.json
{
  "name": "pollme",
  "version": "1.0.0",
  "description": "",
  "main": "server.js",
  "scripts": {
    "test": "echo \"Error: no test specified\" && exit 1"
  },
  "keywords": [
    "Capstone",
    "Project",
    "-",
```

```
    "Practical",
    "Hapi"
  ],
  "author": "",
  "license": "ISC"
}
```

As before, install the dependencies for your project:

@hapi/hapi – The dependency for all your core framework

@hapi/basic – The dependency for all basic authentication

@hapi/joi – The dependency for all Joi validation

mysql2, sequelize – For all database work

nodemon – For monitoring the server

All of these have been introduced in the chapters that went by. Some dependencies do get moved in between their packages, and while you're running an app, the console can give a very helpful dump to tell you the actual path you need to save.

Here's the CLI command list:

```
>npm install --save @hapi/hapi
>npm install --save @hapi/basic
>npm install --save @hapi/joi
>npm install --save mysql2
>npm install --save sequelize
>npm install -g nodemon
```

We then step into modeling the database.

Modeling the Database

Our Sequelize model assumes that the tables exist. We haven't taken the course of modeling tables that don't exist – the option is provided for us by Sequelize. Check the docs for more information. We briefly touch the topic in the Appendix at the end of the book.

As before, keep the same structure as in the app called "hapi-database-orm-full" (see Figure 7-7). It's included in the source code for Chapter 6. Here is a snapshot again.

Figure 7-7. *Code Folder Structure*

In the first few pages of this section (and trust us this chapter is going to get long), we'll be demonstrating the following important concepts:

- Validators and constraints

- Hooks

- Sequelize WHERE clause

- Sequelize INSERT

- Password encryption

- Timestamps in Sequelize

Registering the User

We now move on to the user schema for the database read and writes. Our file in the model folder, called **User.js,** can be modified as seen in Listing 7-2.

Listing 7-2. Modifying Our Model File for the Users Table

```
1.   const dataTypes = require('sequelize');
2.   const bcrypt = require('bcrypt'); //npm install --save bcrypt
3.   var user;
4.   module.exports = function(connection){
```

```
5.    user = connection.define('user', {
6.    user_id:
7.    {
          primaryKey: true,
          allowNull: false,
          type: dataTypes.INTEGER,
          autoIncrement: true
8.    },
9.    first_name: {
              type: dataTypes.STRING,
              allowNull: false },
10.   last_name: {
              type: dataTypes.STRING,
              allowNull: false },
11.   email: {
              type: dataTypes.STRING,
              allowNull: false
12.   },
13.       password:{
          type: dataTypes.STRING,
              allowNull: false
14.       }
15.       },{
16.       timestamps : false,
17.       hooks : { //notice how we encrypt the password
18.       beforeCreate : (user , options) => {
          {
          user.password = user.password && user.password != "" ? bcrypt.
          hashSync(user.password, 10) : "";
          console.log("Before Creating The User");
          }
19.       }
20.   }
21.   })
22.   return user;
23.   }
```

Ensuring Valid Data Entry

Validators and Constraints

The Sequelize documentation (`https://sequelize.org/master/manual/validations-and-constraints.html`) states that

> *Validations are checks performed in the Sequelize level, in pure JavaScript. They can be arbitrarily complex if you provide a custom validator function, or can be one of the built-in validators offered by Sequelize. If a validation fails, no SQL query will be sent to the database at all.*

> *On the other hand, constraints are rules defined at SQL level. The most basic example of constraint is a Unique Constraint. If a constraint check fails, an error will be thrown by the database and Sequelize will forward this error to our error handler.*

Let's see the `allowNull` and unique keywords and how they're a validator and constraint, respectively:

`allowNull: false` is a validator (and a constraint; we'll take a look in a moment).

`unique: true` is a constraint.

Revisiting the preceding definition, if you pass a null value for a field with an `allowNull: false` validator, your query isn't sent to the database at all. If you pass an already existing value, for a `unique: true` constraint, you get a `SequelizeUniqueConstraintError`. The Sequel query is performed, and this error is passed from the database to our error handler.

In Listing 7-3, we've given quite a few validators you could use. And while this saves you time from looking into reference docs online, an insight would show you the validator called `notNull`. What we gave earlier was `allowNull`, which as we mentioned is the only check in Sequelize that is a mix of a *validation* and a *constraint*. If an attempt is made to set null to a field that does not allow null, a `ValidationError` will be thrown without any SQL query being performed.

Listing 7-3. An Example Listing with Built-In Validators, Taken from Sequelize Docs

```
sequelize.define('foo', {
  bar: {
    type: DataTypes.STRING,
    validate: {
```

```
is: /^[a-z]+$/i,              // matches this RegExp
is: ["^[a-z]+$",'i'],         // same as above, but constructing the
                                 RegExp from a string
not: /^[a-z]+$/i,             // does not match this RegExp
not: ["^[a-z]+$",'i'],        // same as above, but constructing the
                                 RegExp from a string
isEmail: true,                // checks for email format (foo@bar.com)
isUrl: true,                  // checks for url format (http://foo.com)
isIP: true,                   // checks for IPv4 (129.89.23.1) or IPv6
                                 format
isIPv4: true,                 // checks for IPv4 (129.89.23.1)
isIPv6: true,                 // checks for IPv6 format
isAlpha: true,                // will only allow letters
isAlphanumeric: true,         // will only allow alphanumeric characters,
                                 so "_abc" will fail
isNumeric: true,              // will only allow numbers
isInt: true,                  // checks for valid integers
isFloat: true,                // checks for valid floating point numbers
isDecimal: true,              // checks for any numbers
isLowercase: true,            // checks for lowercase
isUppercase: true,            // checks for uppercase
notNull: true,                // won't allow null
isNull: true,                 // only allows null
notEmpty: true,               // don't allow empty strings
equals: 'specific value',     // only allow a specific value
contains: 'foo',              // force specific substrings
notIn: [['foo', 'bar']],      // check the value is not one of these
isIn: [['foo', 'bar']],       // check the value is one of these
notContains: 'bar',           // don't allow specific substrings
len: [2,10],                  // only allow values with length between 2
                                 and 10
isUUID: 4,                    // only allow uuids
isDate: true,                 // only allow date strings
isAfter: "2011-11-05",        // only allow date strings after a specific
                                 date
```

```
      isBefore: "2011-11-05",    // only allow date strings before a
                                 //   specific date
      max: 23,                   // only allow values <= 23
      min: 23,                   // only allow values >= 23
      isCreditCard: true,        // check for valid credit card numbers

      // Examples of custom validators:
      isEven(value) {
        if (parseInt(value) % 2 !== 0) {
          throw new Error('Only even values are allowed!');
        }
      }
      isGreaterThanOtherField(value) {
        if (parseInt(value) <= parseInt(this.otherField)) {
          throw new Error('Bar must be greater than otherField.');
        }
      }
    }
  }
});
```

Encrypting Passwords

Hooks

Sequelize enables special filter methods that you can hook into, before, or after a database transaction. The full list of these hooks is given here:

https://github.com/sequelize/sequelize/blob/master/lib/hooks.js

The most common ones are Instance Hooks:

- beforeValidate

- afterValidate/validationFailed

- beforeCreate/beforeUpdate/beforeSave/beforeDestroy

- afterCreate/afterUpdate/afterSave/afterDestroy

Sequelize emits these whenever you're editing a single object (see Listing 7-4).

Listing 7-4. Using Hooks

```
User.beforeCreate(user => {
  if (user.email.includes("@codnostic.com")) {
    throw new Error("Codnostic Domain Not Allowed!");
  }
});
```

Hence Sequelize shows an error as seen in Listing 7-5.

Listing 7-5. The Result of Using the Preceding Hook

```
try {
  await User.create({ email: 'kanika@codnostic.com' });
} catch (error) {
  console.log(error); // Codnostic Domain Not Allowed!
};
```

And Sequelize shows success for the following (Listing 7-6).

Listing 7-6. Another Example Where the Hook beforeCreate Defined Earlier Is Used

```
try {
  await User.create({ email: 'kanika@gmail.com' });
  console.log("success");
} catch (error) {
  console.log(error); // Doesn't happen
};
```

Check line number 17 in Listing 7-2. It's reiterated in the following. We've used hooks for hashing our password, since saving a password in plain text is bad practice. Here's the snippet (Listing 7-7) that does the magic.

Listing 7-7. Hooks Used for Hashing Passwords

```
hooks : {
        beforeCreate : (user , options) => {
            {
```

```
        user.password = user.password && user.password != "" ?
        bcrypt.hashSync(user.password, 10) : "";
        console.log("Before Creating The User");
    }
}
```

We pass it the user object, and if the user.password property is not empty, we return a user.password that is hashed.

To the file userUtil.js, add the snippet in Listing 7-8.

Listing 7-8. Snippet for Registering a User in the Util Class

```
async function registerUser(firstNameP, lastNameP, passwordP, emailP) {
    console.log("Inside utils::userUtil.js::registerUser");
    var result = {};
    try{
    var regUser = await user.build({
        first_name:firstNameP,
        last_name:lastNameP,
        password:passwordP,
        email:emailP
    }).save();
    await user.sync();
    result = regUser.toJSON();
    }
    catch(err)
    {
        console.error(err + "Inside utils::userUtil.js");
        throw (err);
    }
    return {result};
}
```

The code in bold shows that you can build an object and call the save() method followed by the user.sync()method to complete the persistence. We return the JSON representation of the object returned from the build method. Read more about saving instances here: https://sequelize.org/master/manual/model-instances.html#creating-an-instance.

Call this in the controller as seen in Listing 7-9.

Listing 7-9. UserController.js – Call the Preceding Utility Method

```
async function registerUser(firstNameP, lastNameP, passwordP, emailP) {
    console.log("Inside controllers::userController.js::registerUser");
    var response = {}
    try
    {
        response = await utils.userUtil.registerUser(firstNameP,
        lastNameP, passwordP, emailP)
    }catch(err)
    {console.error("Inside Controller Reg Err", err); response = err.
    errors; throw err};
    return {response};
 }
```

Let us now create a request to process all of this (Listing 7-10).

Listing 7-10. Creating a Request in the Routes File

```
{
    method: 'POST',
    path: '/user/create',
    config: {
        description: 'Register users',
        tags: ['api', 'users'],
        validate: {
            payload: joi.object({
                firstName: joi.string().required(),
                lastName: joi.string().required(),
                email: joi.string().email({multiple:true}).required(),
                password: joi.string().required(),
            })
        }
    },
    handler: async function (request, h) {
```

```
        var registerUser = {};
        try
        {
            registerUser = await controllers.userController.
            registerUser(request.payload.firstName,
                    request.payload.lastName, request.payload.
                    password,request.payload.email ).then(
                            function(registerUser) {
return registerUser; }).catch(err=>{console.log("Throw Err From Handler");
throw err});}
catch(err)
            {
            console.error('Ouch in Handler', err);
            return {response:err.errors}
            }
            return registerUser;
        }//end of handler
}//end of route
```

The preceding listing does nothing special; it creates a route, validates it as we discussed before in Chapter 5, and then passes it to the handler. The handler calls the controller, and the utility is processed according to our preceding code. Figure 7-8 shows a request to create a user, and Figure 7-9 shows the corresponding response. Let's take a look.

Figure 7-8. *Creating a User – the Request*

You'll get this response in POSTMAN.

Body   Cookies   Headers (5)   Test Results   Status: 200 OK

Pretty   Raw   Preview   Visualize   JSON ▼   ⇥

```
1  {
2      "response": {
3          "result": {
4              "user_id": 60,
5              "first_name": "Jagpreet",
6              "last_name": "Sharma",
7              "password": "$2b$10$a6/DqjrPXMYpMcWKfe/Uy.AvfSXg/sG/BfCzv51X4zz31ROsZuAE6",
8              "email": "sales1234@codnodfddfsticity.com"
9          }
10     }
11 }
```

Figure 7-9. *Response for Create User API*

Fetching a User

We now explore basic ways of fetching, introducing the WHERE clause and also exploring fetch by primary key, as a native offering from Sequelize. Here we go.

The Sequelize WHERE Clause

Listing 7-11. Fetching Columns Without the WHERE Clause

```
try{
    listUsers = await models.usersModel.findAll({
        attributes: ['firstName', 'lastName']
    })

}catch(err)
{
    console.error(err);
    throw err;
}
```

We gave a simple glimpse of a `Sequelize` fetch in Chapter 6. Add some curry. Here we go! Let's code our `userUtil.js` again. Add the following snippet.

Listing 7-12. Modifying the WHERE Clause: **[Op.like] and [Op.and]**

```
async function findUsers(firstNameP, emailP) {
    console.log("Inside utils::userUtil.js::fetchUsers");

    try{
    if(emailP=="")
    {
        listUsers = await user.findAll({
        attributes: ['first_name', 'last_name', 'email'],
         where: {
                first_name:
                    {
                    [Op.like]:firstNameP
                    }
                }
        })
    }else if(emailP!="")
        {
        listUsers = await user.findAll({
            attributes: ['first_name', 'last_name', 'email'],
             where: {
                [Op.and]: [
                    {
                    first_name:
                        {
                        [Op.like]:firstNameP
                        }},
                    {
                    email:emailP
                    }
                    ]
                    }
            })
        }
    }catch(err)
```

```
    {
        console.error(err);
        throw err;
    }
    return {listUsers:listUsers};
    }
```

We've highlighted **[Op.like] and [Op.and]** to show the WHERE clause. If you run the following in POSTMAN

```
http://localhost:8000/findUsers/Kanika/kanika@codnostic.com
```

you get a response like the following.

Listing 7-13. Response for Fetch Users Service

```
{
    "response": {
        "listUsers": [
            {
                "first_name": "Kanika",
                "last_name": "Sud",
                "email": "kanika@codnostic.com"
            }
        ]
    }
}
```

You've got a dump on the console, which says the following.

Listing 7-14. The Backend Query for the Fetch Users Utility

```
SELECT `first_name`, `last_name`, `email` FROM `users` AS `user` WHERE
(`user`.`first_name` LIKE 'Kanika' AND `user`.`ema
il` = 'kanika@codnostic.com');
```

As you can see, the two operators **[Op.like] and [Op.and]** translated here as LIKE and AND.

A more commonly used approach is when instead of fetching users by email, we fetch by their unique ID instead. The code would then look like this:

```
async function fetchUserById(id) {
    var userById = await user.findByPk(id);
    if (userById === null) {
      return null;
    } else {
      return userById;
    }
}
```

Note how cleanly Sequelize uses user.findByPk to find the user by the primary key. It's a very useful method, and we again recommend going through the Sequelize docs and using the methods, as much as you can, in as many different scenarios. We have used both the approaches in industry-relevant scenarios, and while the latter is more ideal when searching in the back end of an application, the former is applicable when the consumer of the API doesn't know the ID (like the end user of a mobile app).

We now move on to the next section of this product, authenticating a user and protecting services by the token bearer.

Authenticating a User: Statelessness Revisited

Chapter 1 mentioned the statelessness of REST where each request from client to server must contain all of the information necessary to understand the request and cannot take advantage of any stored context on the server. Therefore, whether a user has logged in or not will be determined by the client and not by any contextual information on the server. This introduces us to the concept of the token bearer.

The token bearer is nothing but a token of making sure that you are logged in, and session sensitive information is not exposed otherwise.

In Chapter 5, the authentication example showed you how the user can be authenticated by using a basic scheme. We promised a look at JWT in later chapters, and so looking at it now adds up in our storyline.

To get you started, here's the link for the npm repository:

```
www.npmjs.com/package/hapi-auth-jwt2
```

And here's the link for a basic understanding of JWT:

```
https://github.com/dwyl/learn-json-web-tokens
```

For most readers, a detailed explanation of JSON web tokens might get complicated at this stage, and so we'll smoothen your ride with our example below:

```
www.yoursite.com/private-content/?token=eyJOeXAiOiJKV1Qi.eyJrZXkiOi.
eUiabuiKv
```

For an authentication scheme that you code yourself, you'll use an algorithm to generate the token yourself, and you'll pass it in between services. There's a great overview on JWT from Atlassian, and a must-read for everybody:

```
https://developer.atlassian.com/cloud/jira/platform/understanding-jwt/
```

What JWT does is it generates a token based on a secret key, containing three separate parts:

1. Header (used to describe the token based on the hashing algorithm used)

2. Payload (the core of the token)

3. Signature (used to verify the token)

You can then add it to the authorization header and pass it between services. Listing 7-15 shows the configuration of JWT in a short snippet.

Listing 7-15. Configuring the JWT Server Auth Strategy

```
server.auth.strategy('jwt', 'jwt', true,
{ key: 'NeverShareYourSecret', // Never Share your secret key
  validate: validate,      // validate function defined above
  verifyOptions: {
    ignoreExpiration: true,    // do not reject expired tokens
    algorithms: [ 'HS256' ]    // specify your secure algorithm
  }
});
```

Listing 7-16 shows the route configuration of JWT in a short snippet.

Listing 7-16. Including the JWT Scheme in Your Routes

```
server.route({
      method: 'GET',
      path: '/restricted',
      options: {
          auth: 'jwt',
      },
      handler: function (request, h) {
          return 'welcome';
      }
   });
```

If you need to disable your JWT scheme, for all routes, you could use the code as follows (Listing 7-17).

Listing 7-17. Disabling the Authentication for Publicly Available Content

```
options: { auth: false }
```

If you need to enable your JWT scheme, for all routes, you could use the code as follows (Listing 7-18).

Listing 7-18. Enabling the Authentication for Publicly Available Content

```
server.auth.default('jwt');
//so JWT auth is required for all routes
```

The Request Flow

The following image (Figure 7-10) describes the role of the hapi-auth-jwt strategy in the hapi ecosystem. It's borrowed from the link *https://github.com/dwyl/hapi-auth-jwt2.*

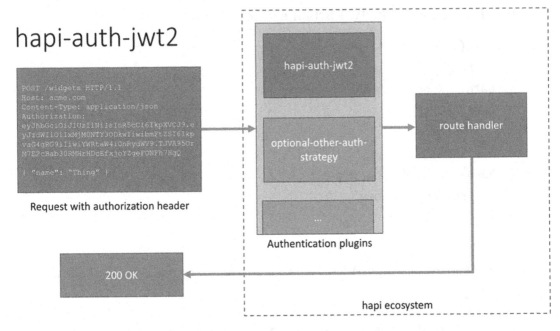

Figure 7-10. *The JWT Authentication Scheme in the hapi Ecosystem*

Creating a Poll Association

For a table to be associated with others, you can enforce it at Sequelize level; or if you have followed this book to the word, you'll be able to enforce associations simply at the database constraint level and avoid any errors. For the intent and purposes of this book, we go by the latter, because it's a tried and tested way, and while Sequelize associations do give you handy accessors to entities, they do get tricky when inserting arrays dynamically in hasMany relations. We still recommend a look at the docs here:

```
https://sequelize.org/master/manual/creating-with-associations.html
```

The preceding link is a good place to start creating entities with Sequelize associations.

By now, we assume that you have been able to understand the MVC structure of the code; and so we skip to adding snippets, instead of showing you entire files. Add the following function to the util layer of your code in order to add and persist a poll object (Listing 7-19).

Listing 7-19. Adding a Poll

```
async function addPoll(pollQuestion, pollLink, userId, optionText){
    console.log("Inside utils::pollUtil.js::addPoll")
    var pollAdded = {};
      try{
          var optArray = optionText.split(',');
          pollAdded = await pollModel.create({
              poll_question:pollQuestion,
              poll_link:pollLink,
              user_id:userId
          });
          for(i = 0; i < optArray.length; i++)
           {
              //build every option
              pollOption = await pollOptionModel.build({
              option_text:optArray[i],
              poll_id:pollAdded.poll_id
              }).save();

           }

         await pollOptionModel.sync();
         await pollModel.sync();

        }catch(err)
        {
            console.error(err);
            throw (err);
        }
        return {"success":true,pollAdded:pollAdded};
}
```

There's no magic here. You've simply added the poll entity and then the poll_
options entity. You sync the pollModel table later, so that if the poll_options are not
added, the poll entity doesn't get added either. Sequelize, by the way, lets you add
associations much easily, but gets a little dirty in case the models are distributed in files.

At any time that you wish to see the created entity on the console, you can just use

```
console.log(JSON.stringify(pollAdded));
```

And you'll get something like this, depending on your POST request:

```
{"poll_id":127,"poll_question":"eq Ass WorksS Last Testsds","poll_
link":"http://www.crona.biz/","user_id":2}
```

And here's the screenshot (Figure 7-11).

Figure 7-11. *Creating a Poll Request*

Delete Poll Associations

Cascade Delete

While you're deleting entries in the master table, you'll want to delete the entries in the child tables, and Sequelize does this for you very cleanly.

Consider the following in our project.

Listing 7-20. Deleting a Poll with Its Options

```
async function deletePoll(id) {

try {

let n = await pollModel.destroy({ where: { poll_id: id } });
    console.log(`number of deleted rows: ${n}`);
    return {"deletedRows" : n};
    } catch (e) {
        console.error(err);
        throw (err);
    }
    return {"deletedRows" : null};
}
```

Without even a mention of pollOptions in Listing 7-20, you were able to delete the poll options. For instance, if you have added the association correctly in the database as we directed you to, your following request to POSTMAN (Figure 7-12) will delete all poll options in poll ID = 47.

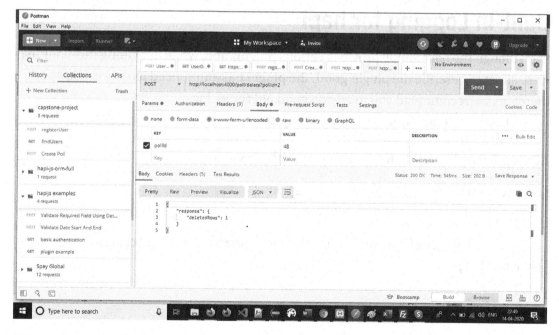

Figure 7-12. *Delete a Poll*

Things to Try Out

We leave it to you to explore the `poll_votes` table. Remember that while casting a vote, a user can cast a vote only for one option in a poll. While many technologists enforce this at the REST API end, you can keep the checks at the UI level and the database level. One drawback of keeping it at the database level is that the constraint will throw an error only after hitting at the database. Therefore, validate the data, rather than throwing verification errors.

The entire code of this application is with the source code of the book. And what's more, you can find accessors to raw queries and others. Make sure you go through the application once.

For users who are excited about hapi and wish to take this one step further, do experiment with Lab – a library that enables automated testing for hapi. Here's the link to get you started:

```
https://hapi.dev/module/lab/
```

What we really need to see is a way of logging and understanding raw queries. And that makes up our last section.

Built-In Logging for hapi

Even though the hapi family provides various plugins and, while beginning this book, we were all set to describe the plugin **good,** the plugin has announced its deprecation and, therefore, we recommend you to rely on good old server logs.

Listing 7-21 shows how to enable logging, listening for any event-labeled log.

Listing 7-21. Listening for Log Events with server.log

```
server.events.on('log', (event, tags) => {

    if (tags.error) {
        console.log(`Server error: ${event.error ? event.error.message :
'unknown'}`);
    }
});
```

Events logged with `server.log()` will emit a log event, and events logged with `request.log()` will emit a request event. This will be an array containing all the logged request events. You must first set the log.collect option to true on the route; otherwise, this array will be empty.

Listing 7-22. Retrieve All Logs

```
server.route({
    method: 'GET',
    path: '/',
    options: {
        log: {
            collect: true
        }
    },
    handler: function (request, h) {

        return 'hello';
    }
});
```

hapi also lets you set a debug option on the server object, and that enables a smooth logging process, without logging code yourself.

In the following line, error is the tag that is configured on the request:

```
const server = Hapi.server({ debug: { request: ['error'] } });
```

Note that larger industry-level applications most effectively ship their logs to products like Splunk, using event collectors like HEC. That level of logging is efficient, and since it's out of the scope of this book, we strongly recommend going through reading material available on the Internet regarding such libraries.

Raw Queries

For many use cases, there will be raw queries required rather than a complex hierarchical maze of various levels. For instance, in a particular case study, where we retrieved followers for a particular user, along with the category of the poll and the profile that he had submitted for government verification, our SQL query became something like this:

```
var sql = "SELECT p.id,p.user_id,p.type,p.poll_type,p.link,p.content,p.
status,p.l_count,p.d_count,p.date_created,p.date_modify,u.verified,u.id as
user_id," +
                " u.username,up.first_name,up.last_name,up.
                description,up.image as user_image" +
                "from polls p join poll_categories pc on p.id =
                pc.poll_id join users u on u.id = p.user_id " +
                "join user_profile up on up.user_id = p.user_id where
                p.status = 1 and pc.category_id = ? and  p.user_id IN
                (5,7) ORDER BY p.id DESC LIMIT 10 ";
```

Now, we have two options, to use Sequelize joins or simply wrap this query in a string and use it through the `sequelize.query` method. The latter is a sensible choice, and here it is:

```
const [results, metadata] = await sequelize.query(sql);
```

That actually brings us to the end of the chapter and the book. And we have covered a huge ground if you look at it in perspective. Here's a short summary.

Summary

In this chapter, we tried introducing a concept with one end of the story of an industrial use case while leaving some of the application to you as well. We covered designing databases with constraints, validators, associations, and cascade operations and creating associated objects; and we also left a trail of alternative Sequelize ways of associations. We ended by looking at built-in logging and raw queries – carefully avoiding plugins where we could.

While our book began with a story of REST APIs, what they mean, and why it's trendy and helpful to code in JavaScript, we subtly moved on to hapi – the new buzzword, with a strong backing. And I quote: "Originally developed to handle Walmart's Black Friday scale, hapi continues to be the proven choice for enterprise-grade backend needs." If you think about it, hapi could quickly become the next backbone of REST APIs with its family of plugins. You should now be equipped with more than sufficient knowledge on how to make REST APIs in hapi, and while you're free or learning, try making the following:

- Making a Doctor Directory REST API (will introduce you to libraries of searching locations)

- Making a Survey API (extend this case study a bit further)

- Making a Job Portal API (will introduce you to multiple layers of CRUD operations)

- Making an Instagram API (security, anyone?)

That list is endless, but should give you enough room for learning and thought. Happy coding!

Appendix

We end our journey with tying up loose ends that can not only fast-track development but also help in a high-level knowledge of what works in the industry, what hitches you might face when bootstrapping your projects, alternatives to POSTMAN, IDEs, plugins, and the like.

NPM

Beginners to the Node.js environment are often aversive to **npm – the Node package manager.** Let's discuss this a little more. When we're writing in Java, my approach is often to go with core features as much as possible, and with Java that's not difficult; even a framework has trillions of features. Dependency management through Maven makes it easy, and we're up and running through including whatever we need on the Java build path.

As for npm, it spoils us for dependencies in Node.js.

npm install does the magic for installing the dependencies. As of writing this book, there are 1,246,729 packages in the repository. The Node ecosystem is constantly growing, and serious Node developers could do well by keeping an eye out on this space and subscribing to which new packages are released:

```
www.npmjs.com/
```

NPM Install Revisited

npm install can be used in three main ways:

```
npm install
```

Just running npm install with no arguments will install everything listed in the dependencies area of the package.json file.

```
npm install <package-name>
```

© Kanika Sud 2020
K. Sud, *Practical hapi*, https://doi.org/10.1007/978-1-4842-5805-7

117

This doesn't add the dependency to the package.json but installs the package.

```
npm install <package-name> --save
```

This adds the dependency to the package.json file and installs the package as well.

Checking for Outdated Dependencies

One built-in way to check which packages are outdated is to run the npm outdated command.

Here it is: `npm outdated`

```
D:\hapijs\ApressBook\pollme>npm outdated
npm ERR! code ETARGET
npm ERR! notarget No matching version found for joi@16.0.1.
npm ERR! notarget In most cases you or one of your dependencies are requesting
npm ERR! notarget a package version that doesn't exist.

npm ERR! A complete log of this run can be found in:
npm ERR!     C:\Users\Kanika Sud\AppData\Roaming\npm-cache\_logs\2020-04-01T21_57_36_686Z-debug.log

D:\hapijs\ApressBook\pollme>
```

This is what it gives on the terminal for any outdated dependency in your project. Another way is the NPM Check Updates module:

```
npm install -g npm-check-updates
```

We won't be covering this, but it's worth a shot when you're working in larger teams.

JSHint and JSLint for Visual Studio

JavaScript can be very evasive in terms of errors. Especially in a promise-based syntax, we generally don't get to know what we might be writing.

JSLint and JSHint come to the rescue in all such cases and are programs that flag suspicious usage in programs written in JavaScript.

Previously, JSLint was the main linting tool for JavaScript. JSHint was just a new fork of JSLint. JSHint has caught up beautifully and is a good option now. Most IDEs now provide plugins that make use of both JSLint and JSHint.

Do refer to the docs here: `https://jshint.com/docs/`

And take a look at what the tool checks for here:

`https://jshint.com/docs/options/`

If you're using Visual Studio, you can get the `jslint` plugin by globally installing it like this:

```
npm install -g jslint
```

For any other IDE, you can use the JSHint package:

```
npm install -g jshint
```

Tracking Patches

An Example for Our Own Code

Sometimes even the latest updates to a library cause problems that you might not be able to catch, because of a bug in the library itself. For this, the dev team releases what is called a **patch.**

As an example, when we set out to writing this book, the Joi validator did not require a wraparound object. It was configured plainly. Listing A-1 shows how we earlier configured a Joi object.

Listing A-1. Joi for Older Versions of hapi

```
config: {
            validate: {
                payload: {
                    date :Joi.date().required()
                }
            }
        },
```

But for hapi 19, the preceding code won't work.

Here's what the console throws:

```
Cannot set uncompiled validation rules without configuring a validator
```

Figure A-1 shows the Joi exception when we use an older version of joi with hapi 19. This shows, how you should be version aware of the libraries you ar

```
Error: Cannot set uncompiled validation rules without configuring a validator
    at new module.exports (D:\hapijs\ApressBook\pollme\node_modules\@hapi\hoek\lib\error.js:23:19)
    at Object.module.exports [as assert] (D:\hapijs\ApressBook\pollme\node_modules\@hapi\hoek\lib\assert.js:20:11)
    at Object.exports.compile (D:\hapijs\ApressBook\pollme\node_modules\@hapi\hapi\lib\validation.js:48:10)
    at module.exports.internals.Route._setupValidation (D:\hapijs\ApressBook\pollme\node_modules\@hapi\hapi\lib\route.js:197:43)
    at new module.exports.internals.Route (D:\hapijs\ApressBook\pollme\node_modules\@hapi\hapi\lib\route.js:122:14)
    at internals.Server._addRoute (D:\hapijs\ApressBook\pollme\node_modules\@hapi\hapi\lib\server.js:498:23)
    at internals.Server.route (D:\hapijs\ApressBook\pollme\node_modules\@hapi\hapi\lib\server.js:491:22)
    at start (D:\hapijs\ApressBook\pollme\server.js:38:12)
```

Figure A-1. *Joi Exception When Used the Old Way*

In fact, when you use the latest of hapi and the latest of Joi, you'll need a wrapper object for the joi config.

Listing A-2. Joi for the Latest Version of hapi

```
validate: {
        params: joi.object({
            firstName: joi.string().required(),
            email: joi.string().email(),
            })
        }
    }
```

The idea to mention this here is that when working on Node.js projects, do keep in mind the code of the modules. If it's not working in spite of being installed and configured, look for patches online.

Swagger
The Benefits of API Documentation

When you're working with APIs, one thing that bothers you most is passing it to the team for API adoption, for better understanding and awareness of the project lifecycle.

In fact API documentation tools have shown major growth in the past few years, and APIs are often designed on such tools before they are coded.

One such tool is **Swagger**:

```
www.npmjs.com/package/hapi-swagger
```

The three commands are

```
npm install hapi-swagger -save
npm install @hapi/inert -save
npm install @hapi/vision -save
```

And you're ready to use Swagger in your hapi application. Listing A-3 shows the modified server file for Swagger.

Listing A-3. Server.js File for Swagger Usage

```
//server.js
const Hapi = require('@hapi/hapi');
const Inert = require('@hapi/inert');
const Vision = require('@hapi/vision');
const HapiSwagger = require('hapi-swagger');
const Pack = require('./package');

(async () => {
    const server = await new Hapi.Server({
        host: 'localhost',
        port: 3000,
    });

    const swaggerOptions = {
        info: {
                title: 'Test API Documentation',
                version: Pack.version,
            },
        };

    await server.register([
        Inert,
        Vision,
        {
            plugin: HapiSwagger,
            options: swaggerOptions
        }
    ]);
```

```
    try {
        await server.start();
        console.log('Server running at:', server.info.uri);
    } catch(err) {
        console.log(err);
    }

    server.route(Routes);
})();
```

Assuming that you've installed the dependencies and modified your server.js file accordingly, check the port on which your app is running and hit the documentation endpoint:

```
http://localhost:8000/documentation
```

Swagger is now enabled!

For any API to show in the docs, you need to tag it thus

```
config:{
            description: 'Register users',
            tags: ['api', 'users']},
```

in the routes file.

So full-fledged route would now look like the following.

Listing A-4. Route with Swagger Enabled

```
    {
        method: 'GET',
         path: '/getUsers',
         config:{
            description: 'Get users',
            tags: ['api', 'users']},
        handler: async function (request, h) {
            try
            {
            var allUsers = controllers.userController.fetchUsers();
                console.log("success");
                return allUsers;
```

```
        }catch(err)
        { console.error('Ouch in getUsers', err); };

    }}
```

And here is the screenshot of Swagger on the browser. Figure A-2 shows what swagger looks like.

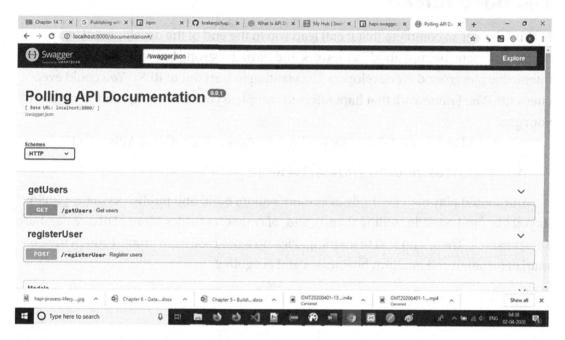

Figure A-2. *Swagger Documentation*

As you can see, the docs look for the HTTP method, use the description in the config, fetch the params or the request body, and render on the docs. Listing A-5 explores the configuration with Swagger inclusive of parameters.

Listing A-5. Config with Swagger and Parameters

```
config:{
        description:"Find User By Name And/Or Email",
        tags: ['api', 'users'],
        validate: {
            params: joi.object({
                firstName: joi.string().required(),
```

```
        email: joi.string().email(),
        })
    }
},
```

The Road Ahead

No book is ever so complete that it can lead you to the end of the development in any framework. hapi, being a good framework and having a strong backing, is an ideal interactive playground for developers just wanting to start out in REST. You could even check the Web Framework that hapi offers to complete your knowledge and strengthen your gap.

You should also look at the following book by Apress for building APIs with Node.js:

`www.apress.com/gp/book/9781484224410`

You should play with methods in authentication, build and publish as many plugins as you like (and consider selling them!), and, of course, consider MongoDB as a database server as well. There's no end to learning. Pick up a use case from around you in the market for small and medium businesses and get going!

Index

A

Application programming
 interface (API), 2
Asynchronous programming
 async/await, 31
 callbacks (*see* Callbacks)
 client servicing, 21
 data-intensive apps, 21
 demonstrating promises, 29, 30
 event loop, 32
 multi-threaded
  environment, 21
 Node.js, 32, 33
 promise syntax, 29
 resolve/reject, 29
 single-threaded language, 22
Authentication
 basic auth, 55, 56
 method, 54
 payload/response, 55
 tab, 56

B

Basic auth
 credential object, 58
 hapi-auth-jwt, 58
 plugin, 57
 validate function, 58
Built-in logging, 112, 113

C

Callbacks
 Ajax, 23
 first-class functions, 22
 home screen change
  content, 24
 loading and reading asynchronous, 22
 setTimeout() function, 25
 syntax, 28
 without code, 26
 without output, 27, 28
Client, 2
Command line interface (CLI), 36

D

Databases
 data-intensive applications, 64
 document-based storage, 63, 64
 multi-server handling, 64
 ORM, 64
 tools, 68, 69
 validation, 64
Designing the solution
 modeling database, 93
 user (*see* User registration)
dotenv utility, 75

E, F

Event loop, 15, 33

© Kanika Sud 2020
K. Sud, *Practical hapi*, https://doi.org/10.1007/978-1-4842-5805-7

G

GET method, 47
    github api, 5
    request/response object, HTTP, 5

H

Handler, 43
hapi
    framework dependencies, 38
    server.js, 38, 39
Hapi.js, 32, 33

I

index.js file, 50
Init method, 42

J, K

Joi, 49
Joi.date() function, 53
JSHint, 118
JSLint, 118
Just-in-time (JIT) compilation, 16

L

loadDoc() function, 30
Loading dependencies, 39, 46

M

Microservice
    architecture, 17
    vs. monolithic architecture, 17
    node.js, 18
Models
    appConfig.js, 75
    config/index.js, 76
    controller folder, 73
    controller layer, 82
    folder structure, 71, 73
    index file, 78
    index.js file, 80
    layers, 71
    main routes file, 81
    MVC app, 72
    remove asynchronous
        programming, 83
    routes/index.js, 73
    Sequelize, 84
    server.js, 74, 77
    user model exported, 79
    utility layer, 81
    utils folder, 73
    workflow, 74
MongoDB, 124
Multiple background processing, 15

N, O

Node.js
    asynchronous programming model, 15
    dev community, 13
    event log, 15
    event loop, 16
    frameworks, 18, 19
    installation, 35, 36
    productivity, 16
    single-threaded asynchronous
        model, 19
    Spring Boot, 14
    traditional models, 15
Nodemon, 69, 70
Node package manager (NPM)
    framework, 117

installation, 117

modules, 118

outdated dependencies, 118

P

package.json file, 45, 49

Package-lock.json, 46

Plugin/module.exports, 59–62

Poll association

cascade delete, 110, 111

creation, 108–110

Polls

constraint, 89

ER diagram, 88, 90

main entities, 86

mind map, 87

MySQL, 87

package.json, 91, 92

registered users table, 91

table, 89

terminology, 88

vote table, 90

poll_votes table, 112

POST method

CRUD operation, 8

HTTP object, 8

response headers, 10

response object, 9

Process object, 44, 45

Q

Query parameter approach

coherence, 7

initial purpose, 7

readability, 7

search engine-friendly, 7

R

Representational state

transfer (REST), 1, 2

request.auth.options config, 58

REST APIs

addressing resources, 6

application layer protocols, 11

design, 2

GET method, 4, 6

hapi, 115

HTTP, 3

mobile app, 2

POST method, 8–10

query parameter approach, 7

representational state transfer, 2

request cycle, 4

resource users/filtering, 3

stateless constraint, 10

Routes

handler function, 43

handler in config, 44

method, 43

path parameters, 44

table, 43

S

Sequelize

configuration, 67, 68

database connection, 65–67

data-driven app, 64

sequelize.query method, 114

Server

folder structure, 38

npm init Utility, 37

object, 40, 41

optional configuration object, 42

package.json file, 37

server.auth.strategy function, 57
server.js file, 50
server.route method, 75
setTimeout() function, 25
Spring Boot, 14
start() method, 42, 57
Stateless constraint, 10
Swagger
    API documentation, 120, 123
    parameters, 123
    route enabled, 122
    Server.js File, 121, 122

T

then() method call, 30
Tracking patches, 119, 120

U

User authentication
    disabling, 107

    enabling, 107
    JWT, 105
    request flow, 108
    route configuration, 107
    server auth strategy, 106
    statelessness, 105
    token, 106
User registration
    encrypting passwords, 97–100
    modification, 93, 94
    validators/constraints, 95–97
    WHERE clause, 102, 104, 105

V, W, X, Y, Z

Validation
    date, Joi, 53
    Joi.ref(), 54
    recommended libraries, 51
    request blocks, 53
    routes/index.js file, 52
V8 javaScript engine, 16